W9-ATY-659

Teen Rights and Freedoms

Tobacco and Smoking

Teen Rights and Freedoms

Tobacco and Smoking

Roman Espejo
Book Editor

GREENHAVEN PRESS
A part of Gale, Cengage Learning

Farmington Hills, Mich • San Francisco • New York • Waterville, Maine
Meriden, Conn • Mason, Ohio • Chicago

Elizabeth Des Chenes, *Director, Content Strategy*
Cynthia Sanner, *Publisher*
Douglas Dentino, *Manager, New Product*

WCN: 01-100-101

For more information, contact:
Greenhaven Press
27500 Drake Rd.
Farmington Hills, MI 48331-3535
Or you can visit our Internet site at gale.cengage.com.

Articles in Greenhaven Press anthologies are often edited for length to meet page requirements. In addition, original titles of these works are changed to clearly present the main thesis and to explicitly indicate the author's opinion. Every effort is made to ensure the Greenhaven Press accurately reflects the original intent of the authors. Every effort has been made to trace the owners of copyrighted material.

LIBRARY OF CONGRESS CATALOGING-IN-PUBLICATION DATA

Tobacco and smoking / Roman Espejo, book editor.
pages cm. -- (Teen rights and freedoms)
Includes bibliographical references and index.
ISBN 978-0-7377-6405-5 (hardcover)
1. Smoking. 2. Teenagers--Tobacco use. I. Espejo, Roman, 1977-
HV5740.T58 2014
362.29'6--dc23

2013036324

Printed in the United States of America
1 2 3 4 5 6 7 18 17 16 15 14

Contents

Foreword

> *"In the truest sense freedom cannot be bestowed, it must be achieved."*
>
> *Franklin D. Roosevelt, September 16, 1936*

The notion of children and teens having rights is a relatively recent development. Early in American history, the head of the household—nearly always the father—exercised complete control over the children in the family. Children were legally considered to be the property of their parents. Over time, this view changed, as society began to acknowledge that children have rights independent of their parents, and that the law should protect young people from exploitation. By the early twentieth century, more and more social reformers focused on the welfare of children, and over the ensuing decades advocates worked to protect them from harm in the workplace, to secure public education for all, and to guarantee fair treatment for youths in the criminal justice system. Throughout the twentieth century, rights for children and teens—and restrictions on those rights—were established by Congress and reinforced by the courts. Today's courts are still defining and clarifying the rights and freedoms of young people, sometimes expanding those rights and sometimes limiting them. Some teen rights are outside the scope of public law and remain in the realm of the family, while still others are determined by school policies.

Each volume in the Teen Rights and Freedoms series focuses on a different right or freedom and offers an anthology of key essays and articles on that right or freedom and the responsibilities that come with it. Material within each volume is drawn from a diverse selection of primary and secondary sources—journals, magazines, newspapers, nonfiction books, organization newsletters, position papers, speeches, and government documents, with a particular emphasis on Supreme Court and lower court decisions. Volumes also include first-person narratives from young people and others involved in teen rights issues, such as parents and educators. The material is selected and arranged to highlight all the major social and legal controversies relating to the right or freedom under discussion. Each selection is preceded by an introduction that provides context and background. In many cases, the essays point to the difference between adult and teen rights, and why this difference exists.

Many of the volumes cover rights guaranteed under the Bill of Rights and how these rights are interpreted and protected in regard to children and teens, including freedom of speech, freedom of the press, due process, and religious rights. The scope of the series also encompasses rights or freedoms, whether real or perceived, relating to the school environment, such as electronic devices, dress, Internet policies, and privacy. Some volumes focus on the home environment, including topics such as parental control and sexuality.

Numerous features are included in each volume of Teen Rights and Freedoms:

- An annotated **table of contents** provides a brief summary of each essay in the volume and highlights court decisions and personal narratives.
- An **introduction** specific to the volume topic gives context for the right or freedom and its impact on daily life.
- A brief **chronology** offers important dates associated with the right or freedom, including landmark court cases.
- **Primary sources**—including personal narratives and court decisions—are among the varied selections in the anthology.
- **Illustrations**—including photographs, charts, graphs, tables, statistics, and maps—are closely tied to the text and chosen to help readers understand key points or concepts.

- An annotated list of **organizations to contact** presents sources of additional information on the topic.
- A **for further reading** section offers a bibliography of books, periodical articles, and Internet sources for further research.
- A comprehensive subject **index** provides access to key people, places, events, and subjects cited in the text.

Each volume of Teen Rights and Freedoms delves deeply into the issues most relevant to the lives of teens: their own rights, freedoms, and responsibilities. With the help of this series, students and other readers can explore from many angles the evolution and current expression of rights both historic and contemporary.

Introduction

The smoking age in the United States is currently eighteen in all but four states: Alabama, Alaska, New Jersey, and Utah, where it is nineteen. In addition, several counties in New York have higher smoking ages, and New York City raised the age to twenty-one in 2013. The smoking age was established nationally when former president George H.W. Bush signed the Alcohol, Drug Abuse, and Mental Health Administration Reorganization Act into law in 1992. Specifically, the Synar Amendment (named after sponsoring Congressman Mike Synar) required by 1995 that each state enforce laws prohibiting the sale and distribution of tobacco products to persons under eighteen. Furthermore, states must randomly inspect and assess vendor compliance to these laws and submit annual reports on their findings to the US Secretary of Health and Human Services. The aim of the amendment is to cut underage purchases to 20 percent or less in each state annually; those in noncompliance face losing a percentage of federal funding for substance abuse programs. The Substance Abuse and Mental Health Services Administration, which supervises implementation of the Synar Amendment, claims that tobacco sales to minors reached a low of 8.5 percent in the fiscal year of 2011.

Along with such efforts, the tobacco industry has long been accused of targeting minors as consumers. In a landmark lawsuit brought by the US Department of Justice, the *United States v. Philip Morris* (2006), several companies—including Philip Morris, R.J. Reynolds, Lorillard, Brown and Williamson, and American Tobacco Company—were found guilty of tracking the behavior of youths to create marketing strategies and advertising campaigns. In the US District Court for the District of Columbia's opinion, Senior Judge Gladys Kessler presented detailed examples for these companies' activities, such as sponsoring school athletics and scholarships and intentionally maintaining cigarette prices to remain affordable to the youngest consumers. "Defendants used their knowledge of young people to create highly sophisticated and appealing marketing campaigns targeted to lure them into starting smoking and later becoming nicotine addicts," she argued. Also, Kessler cited attempts to use imagery and packaging to appeal to underage consumers and portray smoking as cool and grown up. "Above all, Defendants have burnished the image of their youth brands to convey rugged independence, rebelliousness, love of life, adventurousness, confidence, self-assurance, and belonging to the 'in' crowd," she declared.

Three years later, President Barack Obama signed the 2009 Family Smoking Prevention and Tobacco Control Act into law. It recognizes that "virtually all new users of tobacco products are under the minimum legal age to purchase such products" and "tobacco advertising and marketing contribute significantly to the use of nicotine-containing tobacco products by adolescents." The law introduced a host of new restrictions to reduce tobacco sales and access to minors, including the requirement of face-to-face sales (only permitting vending machines and self-service displays in all-adult establishments), a ban on packages with fewer than twenty cigarettes, and limitations on the colors and designs of packaging and advertisements. The same year, a federal ban on flavored cigarettes followed, with health officials alleging that flavorings like chocolate, vanilla, and clove heighten the appeal of smoking to children and adolescents.

Over the past decade, bills have been introduced—but not yet passed—in a number of states to raise the smoking age to twenty-one. According to the Centers for Disease Control and Prevention and an analysis from the American Lung Association, 68 percent of smokers began when they were eighteen and younger. "If current tobacco use patterns persist, an estimated 6.4 million current child smokers will eventually die prematurely from a smoking-related disease," claims the American

Lung Association. Due to such findings, antismoking advocates believe that increasing the legal age to buy tobacco products will help protect human health and combat nicotine addiction. "Not only does it reduce the number of life-years available for tobacco use (and of course, the longer a person uses tobacco, the higher the risk of developing severe health consequences), but delays in onset are also associated with a higher probability of successful cessation efforts later," contends the Tobacco Control Legal Consortium.

Nonetheless, critics believe that raising the smoking age would be ineffective. "All the evidence that's out there shows that it is unenforceable at the age of 18," insists David Privera, a physician and member of the California Medical Association. "It will be utterly unenforceable at 21." Raising the smoking age is also viewed as an infringement of young people's rights. "I think that people are going to wonder whether 18-year-olds who can join the armed forces should have the right to smoke and make that choice on their own," observed the late California assemblyman Keith Richman.

When the US Surgeon General officially linked smoking to lung cancer and other serious conditions in 1964, it catalyzed battles for regulating the tobacco industry. Decades later, these conflicts continue to impact the nation. Drawing from court opinions, editorials, and other sources, *Teen Rights and Freedoms: Tobacco and Smoking* examines issues surrounding tobacco use in the context of youths' lives and liberties.

Chronology

January 11, 1964 The US Surgeon General releases its Advisory Committee Report on Smoking and Health, linking cigarettes to lung cancer, bronchitis, and other diseases for the first time. The report declared that "cigarette smoking is a health hazard of sufficient importance in the United States to warrant appropriate remedial action."

July 27, 1965 The Federal Cigarette Labeling and Advertising Act is enacted, requiring health warnings on cigarette packaging.

April 1, 1970 The Public Health Cigarette Smoking Act is signed into law, requiring health warnings on cigarette packaging to be from the US Surgeon General, extending the warnings to any print advertisements, and banning cigarette commercials from television and radio.

September 10, 1973 An amendment to the Federal Cigarette Labeling and Advertising Act, the Little Cigar Act, is passed, which bans cigar commercials from television and radio.

1975 Minnesota becomes the first state to restrict smoking in the workplace with the passage of its Clean Indoor Air Act.

October 12, 1984 The Comprehensive Smoking Education Act of 1984 is enacted, requiring cigarette packaging and print advertisements to carry four rotating health warnings from the US Surgeon General.

February 27, 1986 The Comprehensive Smokeless Tobacco Health Education Act of 1986 is passed, requiring smokeless tobacco packaging and print advertisements to carry three rotating health warnings.

July 10, 1992 The Alcohol, Drug Abuse, and Mental Health Administration Reorganization Act is signed into law. It includes the Synar Amendment, which requires that all states enact laws banning the sale or distribution of tobacco products to minors by 1995.

July 13, 1997 Congress passes legislation to ban smoking on domestic airline flights two hours or less. Two years later, the ban is extended to flights six hours or less.

January 1, 1998 California becomes the first state to ban smoking in most bars and casinos.

March 1, 2000 The US Supreme Court decides in *FDA* v. *Brown & Williamson Tobacco Corp.* that the US Food and Drug Administration does not have the power to regulate tobacco products.

August 17, 2006 The US District Court rules in *United States v. Philip Morris* that tobacco companies have targeted youths in their advertising and marketing campaigns and violated the Racketeer Influenced and Corrupt Organizations Act.

June 22, 2009 The Family Smoking Prevention and Tobacco Control Act is signed into law. It extends the authority of the FDA to regulate tobacco, effectively reversing the Supreme Court's 2000 decision.

June 23, 2009 The Missouri Court of Appeals finds in *City of Kansas City v. Carlson* that a municipal ordinance prohibiting smoking in bars is not in conflict with the state statute that does not define such establishments as public areas.

Viewpoint 1

> "The so-called 'right to smoke' is actually a smokescreen."

Smoking Is Not a Constitutional Right

Samantha K. Graff

In the following viewpoint, Samantha K. Graff argues that smoking is not protected by the US Constitution. The due process clause, which prohibits the government from restricting individual liberty without due process of law, does not include the choice to smoke, she contends, and the right to privacy only relates to reproductive and family decisions. The equal protection clause does not protect smokers as a category of people, adds Graff, and only extends to immutable characteristics such as race, national origin, and gender. Graff is a staff attorney at Public Health Law and Policy, a project of the Public Health Institute in Oakland, California.

Smoking is the leading cause of preventable death in the United States. More than 12 million premature deaths over the past 40 years were attributable to smoking. Today, smoking causes approximately 438,000 deaths each year and results in over $167 bil-

Samantha K. Graff, "There Is No Constitutional Right to Smoke: 2008," second edition, Tobacco Control Legal Consortium, 2008.

lion in annual health-related economic losses. Smoking not only injures nearly every organ of the smoker's body, but it inflicts considerable damage on nonsmokers. Exposure to secondhand smoke is estimated to kill approximately 50,000 non-smokers in the United States each year.

In an attempt to limit the extraordinary harm that tobacco smoke inflicts on individuals and communities, advocates across the country are supporting enactment of state and local smoke-free laws. These advocates have seen their efforts rewarded with a wave of state and local workplace restrictions that prohibit smoking in offices, restaurants and bars. Moreover, various cities have passed smoking restrictions that cover targeted locations, such as playgrounds, parks, beaches, and public transit vehicles. In addition, some local government agencies, such as police and fire departments, have adopted policies requiring job applicants or employees to refrain from smoking both on and off the job. Advocates promoting smoke-free legislation often encounter opponents who make the ominous legal-sounding argument: "You are trampling on my right to smoke." The purpose of this law synopsis is to debunk the argument that smokers have a special legal right to smoke.

If there were a legal justification for a special right to smoke, it would come from the U.S. Constitution. The Constitution lays out a set of civil rights that are specially protected, in that they generally cannot be abrogated by federal, state, county and municipal laws. Section I of this law synopsis explains that neither the Due Process Clause nor the Equal Protection Clause of the Constitution creates a right to smoke. As a result, the Constitution leaves the door wide open for smoke-free laws and other tobacco-related laws that are rationally related to a legitimate government goal. Section II highlights two types of state laws that may create a limited right to smoke. Section II shows that in the absence of a constitutionally protected right to smoke, advocates can seek to amend or repeal these laws, thus taking away any safeguards the laws afford to smokers.

There Is No Constitutional Right to Smoke

Constitutional rights are specially protected, so that laws generally cannot take them away. If a law appears to interfere with a constitutional right, those whose rights are affected can challenge that law in court. A court will invalidate the law if it finds that the law improperly treads on a constitutional right. Constitutional rights include the right to freedom of speech, freedom of religion, due process of law, and equal protection under the law.

The Constitution does not explicitly mention smoking. Therefore, if there were a constitutional right to smoke, it would have to fall under the umbrella of one of the recognized constitutional rights. People who claim a right to smoke usually rely on one of two arguments: (1) that smoking is a personal liberty specially protected by the Due Process Clause, or (2) that the Equal Protection Clause extends special protection to smokers as a group. This section explains that neither of these claims is legally valid. Since smoking is not a specially protected constitutional right, the Constitution does not bar the passage of local, state, or federal smoke-free laws and other restrictions on smoking.

Smoking Is Not a Specially Protected Liberty

Proponents of smokers' rights often claim that the government should not be able to pass smoke-free laws because smoking is a personal choice that falls under the constitutional right to liberty. However, the constitutional right to liberty does not shield smokers from smoke-free legislation.

The Due Process Clause of the Constitution prohibits the government from depriving individuals of liberty without "due process of law." This means that a legislative body must have an adequate justification for passing a law that affects someone's liberty. So, for example, a smoker might challenge a smoke-free workplace law in court if she believes that the law violates the

Finding Legal Protection from Secondhand Smoke

Nonsmokers who live in areas where legislation does not adequately protect them from secondhand smoke can utilize other legal recourses to find protection. Unfortunately, pursuing this strategy usually requires finding an attorney who is willing to represent you. Some attorneys may be willing to accept your case on a contingency basis, in which they will only be paid in the event that you win your case. However, knowing that there are precedents in favor of nonsmokers may be enough to persuade employers and business owners to voluntarily adopt policies that protect nonsmoking employees and customers. Employers in particular are becoming more and more susceptible to liability for not providing a smokefree workplace and should be willing to do whatever it takes to avoid such liability.

Americans for Nonsmokers' Rights, "Rights of Nonsmokers," January 2003.

Due Process Clause because it takes away her liberty by stopping her from smoking at work without an adequate justification.

To assess whether a given law is based on an adequate justification, a court will look at the individual and governmental interests at stake. The criteria a court uses become more demanding as the individual interest at stake becomes more substantial. In most cases, courts require that a law be "rationally related" to a "legitimate" government goal. This requirement sets a very low bar for the government: a law will be considered constitutional so long as the law is not completely irrational or arbitrary.

In some special cases, however, courts set a much higher bar for the government. This happens when a law restricts a type of liberty that is specially protected by the Constitution. Very few types of liberty are specially protected by the Constitution. The "fundamental right to privacy" is one category of liberty that does receive special constitutional protection. Smokers' rights proponents latch onto this fundamental right to privacy, arguing that smoking is a private choice about which the government should have no say. However, the U.S. Supreme Court has held only that the fundamental right to privacy relates to an individual's decisions about reproduction and family relationships. Activities that are specially protected under the fundamental right to privacy include marriage, procreation, abortion, contraception, and the raising and educating of children. The fundamental right to privacy does not include smoking. In the words of one court, "There is no more a fundamental right to smoke cigarettes than there is to shoot up or snort heroin or cocaine or run a red-light."

It is worth noting that in addition to the U.S. Constitution, most state constitutions include a fundamental right to privacy. In some state constitutions, the fundamental right to privacy is broader than that in the U.S. Constitution. However, a thorough search of case law reveals no current court decision holding that smoking falls within a state constitution's fundamental right to privacy.

In fact, several courts have specifically ruled that smoking does not fall under a federal and/or state constitutional right to privacy—even where smoking in private is concerned. For example, in a 1987 Oklahoma case, a federal appellate court considered an Oklahoma City fire department regulation requiring trainees to refrain from cigarette smoking at all times. The lawsuit arose because a trainee took three puffs from a cigarette during an off-duty lunch break, and he was fired that afternoon for violating the non-smoking rule. The trainee sued, asserting that "although there is no specific constitutional right to smoke, it is implicit [in the Constitution] that he has a right of liberty or privacy in the conduct of his private life, a right to be let alone, which includes the right to smoke." The court disagreed and distinguished smoking from the specially protected constitutional privacy rights. Since smoking is not a fundamental privacy right, the court ruled that the regulation could remain on the books since it was rationally related to the legitimate government goal of maintaining a healthy firefighting force.

Similarly, in 1995, a Florida court considered a North Miami city regulation requiring applicants for municipal jobs to certify in writing that they had not used tobacco in the preceding year. The regulation was challenged in court by an applicant for a clerk-typist position who was removed from the pool of candidates because she was a smoker. She claimed that the regulation violated her right to privacy under the federal and state constitutions. The court found that "the 'right to smoke' is not included within the penumbra of fundamental rights" specially protected by the U.S. Constitution. The court also found that, although the fundamental right to privacy in the Florida constitution covers more activities than the fundamental right to privacy in the U.S. Constitution, a job applicant's smoking habits are not among the activities specially protected by the state constitution's privacy provision. The court ultimately upheld the city regulation because it was rationally related to the legitimate government goal of reducing health insurance costs and increasing productivity.

In a 2002 Ohio case involving custody and visitation of an eight-year-old girl, the court banned the girl's parents from smoking in her presence. The court listed pages of evidence about the harms of secondhand smoke, citing hundreds of articles and reports. The court proceeded to hold that smoking is not a specially protected constitutional right and that the fundamental right to privacy "does not include the right to inflict health-destructive secondhand smoke upon other persons, especially children who have no choice in the matter."

Smokers Are Not Covered by the Equal Protection Clause

The second constitutional claim frequently made by proponents of smokers' rights is that smoke-free laws discriminate against smokers as a group in violation of the Equal Protection Clause of the Constitution. No court has been persuaded by this claim.

The Equal Protection Clause guarantees that people are entitled to "equal protection of the laws." The U.S. Supreme Court has interpreted this to mean that the government cannot pass laws that treat one category of people differently from another category of people without an adequate justification. So, for example, a smoker might bring a lawsuit if he believes that a smoke-free workplace law violates the Equal Protection Clause because the law discriminates against smokers and in favor of nonsmokers without an adequate justification.

In most instances, courts require that a discriminatory law be "rationally related" to a "legitimate" government goal. This requirement is very easy for the government to meet, since a discriminatory law will be upheld so long as it is not totally irrational or arbitrary.

The no smoking sign at the entrance of Battery Park in New York City is indicative of a law passed by the city in 2011 making smoking illegal in all parks. The right to smoke is not protected under the US Constitution and may be legally banned in public spaces. © Emmanuel Dunand/AFP/Getty Images.

In a certain set of cases, however, a court will apply a much stricter requirement. This happens when a law discriminates against a category of people that is entitled to special protection. The Equal Protection Clause gives special protection to very few categories of people. In fact, it only extends special protection to groups based on race, national origin, ethnicity, gender, and (historically) illegitimacy. The groups that receive special protection share "an immutable characteristic determined solely by the accident of birth." Because of this special protection, a law is likely to violate the Constitution if it discriminates against a category of people based on race, national origin, ethnicity, gender, or illegitimacy.

Some people argue that smokers make up a category that deserves special protection against discriminatory laws that restrict their ability to smoke at a time and place of their choosing. However, smokers are not a specially protected group under the Constitution. Smoking is not an "immutable characteristic" because people are not born smokers and smoking, while addictive, is still a behavior that people can stop. Since smokers are not a specially protected group, a smoke-free law that "discriminates" against smokers will not violate the Equal Protection Clause so long as the law is rationally related to a legitimate government goal.

Most state constitutions contain an equal protection clause that mirrors the Equal Protection Clause of the U.S. Constitution. Therefore, smokers' rights proponents who challenge a "discriminatory law" limiting smoking also are unlikely to convince a court that smokers deserve special protection under a state equal protection clause.

A 2004 New York case illustrates how courts react negatively to smokers' claims that they are a specially protected group under the Equal Protection Clause. New York City and New York State enacted laws prohibiting smoking in most indoor places in order to protect citizens from the well-documented harmful effects of secondhand smoke. The challenger argued that the smoking bans violated the Equal Protection Clause because they cast smokers as "social lepers by, in effect, classifying smokers as second class citizens." The court responded that "the mere fact that the smoking bans single out and place burdens on smokers as a group does not, by itself, offend the Equal Protection Clause because there is no . . . basis upon which to grant smokers the status of [a specially protected group]." The court upheld the city and state smoking bans since they were rationally related to the legitimate government goal of protecting the public health.

In a 1986 Wisconsin case, a court considered an equal protection challenge to the newly enacted state Clean Indoor Air Act. The Clean Indoor Air Act prohibited smoking in government buildings with the exception of designated smoking areas. A government employee sued, arguing that it would violate the Equal Protection Clause for his employer to discipline him and his fellow smokers for smoking on the job. Since smokers are not a specially protected category, the court noted that "any reasonable basis for [distinguishing smokers from nonsmokers] will validate the statute. Equal protection of the law is denied only where the legislature has made irrational or arbitrary [distinctions]." The court upheld the Clean Indoor Air Act, finding it was rationally related to the legitimate government goals of minimizing the health and safety risks of smoking.

Smokers are not specially protected by the Constitution. A law that restricts smoking will not violate the Constitution so long as it is rationally related to a legitimate government goal. Courts are likely to uphold most smoke-free laws against due process and equal protection challenges, as long as these laws are enacted to further the legitimate government goal of protecting the public health by minimizing the dangers of tobacco smoke.

Laws Cannot Grant an Irrevocable Right to Smoke

The objective of this law synopsis is to clarify that there is no such thing as a constitutional right to smoke. The Constitution does not stand in the way of state or local laws limiting the ability of citizens to light up at a time and place of their choosing.

The Constitution, however, is not the end of the story. Certain laws can create barriers to the enactment of new smoke-free legislation. At least two types of state laws can impede a comprehensive smoke-free agenda. These laws afford a limited right to smoke under certain circumstances unless and until the laws are amended or repealed. . . .

Often, the greatest barrier to a smoke-free agenda is a state law that preempts local governments in the state from passing legislation that goes farther than the state in restricting smoking. The tobacco industry has lobbied hard for state preemption of local smoke-free laws because it is much easier for the tobacco industry to wield influence with state legislatures than with locally elected officials. Such preemptive state laws can be and frequently are loophole-ridden or otherwise ineffective at protecting the public from exposure to secondhand smoke.

Currently, thirty-one states have laws that either totally or partially preempt local smoke-free legislation. In those states, there is no constitutional right to smoke. However, unless and until the preemptive state laws are amended or repealed, local governments in those states cannot pass laws that go beyond the state smoke-free laws. Advocates who want to push local smoke-free legislation in those states must first work to get rid of state preemption.

The Role of Smoker Protection Laws

In approximately thirty states, so-called "smoker protection laws" are a small barrier to a smoke-free agenda. Smoker protection laws prohibit employers from making employment decisions, such as hiring and firing, based on off-duty conduct that is legal, such as using tobacco during non-work hours and away from the job site. Some smoker protection laws are specific to tobacco use, while others apply to all legal off-duty conduct. Smoker protection laws are enacted to thwart the types of policies adopted by the Oklahoma City fire department and North Miami city... that forbid certain employees from smoking at any time.

Smoker protection laws are not as protective as they sound. They do not create a right to smoke. Nor do they give people license to smoke anywhere at any time. Instead, they merely assure some smokers that their employers will not consider their off-duty tobacco use when making employment decisions.

If advocates in states with smoker protection laws want to promote policies similar to those adopted by the Oklahoma City fire department and North Miami city, they must find an existing exception in the smoker protection law or must lobby to amend or repeal the smoker protection law.

Some states have laws that act as roadblocks to effective smoke-free legislation. However, advocates can work to amend or repeal those laws with confidence that their opponents cannot argue successfully that the advocates are trying to trample on a specially protected right to smoke.

The so-called "right to smoke" is actually a smokescreen. There is no constitutional right to smoke. Therefore, advocates are free to seek enactment of new smoke-free laws or the amendment or repeal of existing laws that harm the public health despite claims by their opponents invoking a right to smoke. So long as proposed smoke-free legislation is rationally related to a legitimate government goal, the Constitution will not stand in the way of its passage. Courts are quick to find that smoke-free legislation is rationally related to a legitimate government goal, since they have long held that protecting the public's health is one of the most essential functions of government.

VIEWPOINT 2

"Congress has clearly precluded the FDA from asserting jurisdiction to regulate tobacco products."

The Food and Drug Administration Cannot Regulate the Tobacco Industry

The Supreme Court's Decision

Sandra Day O'Connor

The Food and Drug Administration (FDA) issued a rule in 1996 defining cigarettes and smokeless tobacco as "drug delivery devices." The goal of the FDA was to further restrict the distribution and sale of the products in order to prevent nicotine addiction and protect children and adolescents. In FDA v. Brown & Williamson Tobacco Corp. *(2000), the US Supreme Court found that the agency lacks the jurisdiction to regulate tobacco. In the following viewpoint, US Supreme Court Justice Sandra Day O'Connor contends that if tobacco products are "devices" that cause adverse health effects and addiction, then the FDA would be required to ban them. Moreover, O'Connor observes, Congress has forbidden the exclusion of tobacco*

Sandra Day O'Connor, *FDA v. Brown & Williamson Tobacco Corp*, US Supreme Court, March 1, 2000.

products from the market and national economy, instead legislating their labeling and advertising to address the associated health problems. O'Connor served as an associate justice of the Supreme Court from 1981 to 2006.

This case involves one of the most troubling public health problems facing our Nation today: the thousands of premature deaths that occur each year because of tobacco use. In 1996, the Food and Drug Administration (FDA), after having expressly disavowed any such authority since its inception, asserted jurisdiction to regulate tobacco products. The FDA concluded that nicotine is a "drug" within the meaning of the Food, Drug, and Cosmetic Act (FDCA or Act), and that cigarettes and smokeless tobacco are "combination products" that deliver nicotine to the body. Pursuant to this authority, it promulgated regulations intended to reduce tobacco consumption among children and adolescents. The agency believed that, because most tobacco consumers begin their use before reaching the age of 18, curbing tobacco use by minors could substantially reduce the prevalence of addiction in future generations and thus the incidence of tobacco-related death and disease.

Regardless of how serious the problem an administrative agency seeks to address, however, it may not exercise its authority "in a manner that is inconsistent with the administrative structure that Congress enacted into law" [*ETSI Pipeline Project v. Missouri* (1988)]. And although agencies are generally entitled to deference in the interpretation of statutes that they administer, a reviewing "court, as well as the agency, must give effect to the unambiguously expressed intent of Congress" [*Chevron U.S.A. Inc. v. Natural Resources Defense Council, Inc.* (1984)]. In this case, we believe that Congress has clearly precluded the FDA from asserting jurisdiction to regulate tobacco products. Such authority is inconsistent with the intent that Congress has expressed in the FDCA's overall regulatory scheme and in the tobacco-specific legislation that it has enacted subsequent to the

FDCA. In light of this clear intent, the FDA's assertion of jurisdiction is impermissible.

The FDA's Determination of Nicotine as a Drug

The FDCA grants the FDA, as the designee of the Secretary of Health and Human Services (HHS), the authority to regulate, among other items, "drugs" and "devices." The Act defines "drug" to include "articles (other than food) intended to affect the structure or any function of the body." It defines "device," in part, as "an instrument, apparatus, implement, machine, contrivance . . . or other similar or related article, including any component, part, or accessory, which is . . . intended to affect the structure or any function of the body." The Act also grants the FDA the authority to regulate so-called "combination products," which "constitute a combination of a drug, device, or biological product." The FDA has construed this provision as giving it the discretion to regulate combination products as drugs, as devices, or as both.

On August 11, 1995, the FDA published a proposed rule concerning the sale of cigarettes and smokeless tobacco to children and adolescents. The rule, which included several restrictions on the sale, distribution, and advertisement of tobacco products, was designed to reduce the availability and attractiveness of tobacco products to young people. A public comment period followed, during which the FDA received over 700,000 submissions, more than "at any other time in its history on any other subject."

On August 28, 1996, the FDA issued a final rule entitled "Regulations Restricting the Sale and Distribution of Cigarettes and Smokeless Tobacco to Protect Children and Adolescents." The FDA determined that nicotine is a "drug" and that cigarettes and smokeless tobacco are "drug delivery devices," and therefore it had jurisdiction under the FDCA to regulate tobacco products as customarily marketed—that is, without manufacturer claims of therapeutic benefit. First, the FDA

A business owner stands beside a cigarette vending machine, which was banned by tobacco regulations from the US Food and Drug Administration (FDA) in 1996. In FDA v. Brown & Williamson Tobacco Corp., *the US Supreme Court ruled that the FDA does not have the authority to regulate tobacco.* © Mike Derer/AP Images.

found that tobacco products "affect the structure or any function of the body" because nicotine "has significant pharmacological effects." Specifically, nicotine "exerts psychoactive, or mood-altering, effects on the brain" that cause and sustain addiction, have both tranquilizing and stimulating effects, and control weight. Second, the FDA determined that these effects were "intended" under the FDCA because they "are so widely known and foreseeable that [they] may be deemed to have been intended by the manufacturers; consumers use tobacco products "predominantly or nearly exclusively" to obtain these effects, and the statements, research, and actions of manufacturers revealed that they "have 'designed' cigarettes to provide pharmacologically active doses of nicotine to consumers." Finally, the agency concluded that cigarettes and smokeless tobacco are "combination products" because, in addition to containing nicotine, they include device components that deliver a controlled amount of nicotine to the body.

Having resolved the jurisdictional question, the FDA next explained the policy justifications for its regulations, detailing the deleterious health effects associated with tobacco use. It found that tobacco consumption was "the single leading cause of preventable death in the United States." According to the FDA, "[m]ore than 400,000 people die each year from tobacco-related illnesses, such as cancer, respiratory illnesses, and heart disease." The agency also determined that the only way to reduce the amount of tobacco-related illness and mortality was to reduce the level of addiction, a goal that could be accomplished only by preventing children and adolescents from starting to use tobacco. The FDA found that 82% of adult smokers had their first cigarette before the age of 18, and more than half had already become regular smokers by that age. It also found that children were beginning to smoke at a younger age, that the prevalence of youth smoking had recently increased, and that similar problems existed with respect to smokeless tobacco. The FDA accordingly concluded that if "the number of children and adolescents who begin tobacco use can be substantially diminished, tobacco-related illness can be correspondingly reduced because data suggest that anyone who does not begin smoking in childhood or adolescence is unlikely ever to begin."

Based on these findings, the FDA promulgated regulations concerning tobacco products' promotion, labeling, and accessibility to children and adolescents. The access regulations prohibit the sale of cigarettes or smokeless tobacco to persons younger than 18; require retailers to verify through photo identification the age of all purchasers younger than 27; prohibit the sale of cigarettes in quantities smaller than 20; prohibit the distribution of free samples; and prohibit sales through self-service displays and vending machines except in adult-only locations. The promotion regulations require that any print advertising appear in a black-and-white, text-only format unless the publication in which it appears is read almost exclusively by adults; prohibit outdoor advertising within 1,000 feet of any public playground or school; prohibit the distribution of any promotional items, such as T-shirts or hats, bearing the manufacturer's brand name; and prohibit a manufacturer from sponsoring any athletic, musical, artistic, or other social or cultural event using its brand name. The labeling regulation requires that the statement, "A Nicotine-Delivery Device for Persons 18 or Older," appear on all tobacco product packages.

The FDA promulgated these regulations pursuant to its authority to regulate "restricted devices." The FDA construed § 353(g)(1) as giving it the discretion to regulate "combination products" using the Act's drug authorities, device authorities, or both, depending on "how the public health goals of the act can be best accomplished." Given the greater flexibility in the FDCA for the regulation of devices, the FDA determined that "the device authorities provide the most appropriate basis for regulating cigarettes and smokeless tobacco." Under 21 U. S. C. § 360j(e), the agency may "require that a device be restricted to sale, distribution, or use . . . upon such other conditions as [the FDA] may prescribe in such regulation, if, because of its potentiality for harmful effect or the collateral measures necessary to its use, [the FDA] determines that there cannot otherwise be reasonable assurance of its safety and effectiveness." The FDA reasoned that its regulations fell within the authority granted by § 360j(e) because they related to the sale or distribution of tobacco products and were necessary for providing a reasonable assurance of safety.

Creating Internal Inconsistencies

Respondents, a group of tobacco manufacturers, retailers, and advertisers, filed suit in United States District Court for the Middle District of North Carolina challenging the regulations. They moved for summary judgment on the grounds that the FDA lacked jurisdiction to regulate tobacco products as customarily marketed, the regulations exceeded the FDA's authority under 21 U. S. C. § 360j(e), and the advertising restrictions violated the First Amendment. The District Court granted respondents' motion in part and denied it in part. The court held that the FDCA authorizes the FDA to regulate tobacco products as customarily marketed and that the FDA's access and labeling regulations are permissible, but it also found that the agency's advertising and promotion restrictions exceed its authority under § 360j(e). The court stayed implementation of the regulations it found valid (except the prohibition on the sale of tobacco products to minors) and certified its order for immediate interlocutory appeal.

The Court of Appeals for the Fourth Circuit reversed, holding that Congress has not granted the FDA jurisdiction to regulate tobacco products. Examining the FDCA as a whole, the court concluded that the FDA's regulation of tobacco products would create a number of internal inconsistencies. Various provisions of the Act require the agency to determine that any regulated product is "safe" before it can be sold or allowed to remain on the market, yet the FDA found in its rulemaking proceeding that tobacco products are "dangerous" and "unsafe." Thus, the FDA would apparently have to ban tobacco products, a result the court found clearly contrary to congressional intent. This apparent anomaly, the Court of Appeals concluded, demonstrates that Congress did not intend to give the FDA authority to regulate tobacco. The court also found that evidence external to the FDCA confirms this conclusion. Importantly, the FDA consistently stated before 1995 that it lacked jurisdiction over tobacco, and Congress has enacted several tobacco-specific statutes fully cognizant of the FDA's position. In fact, the court reasoned, Congress has considered and rejected many bills that would have given the agency such authority. This, along with the absence of any intent by the enacting Congress in 1938 to subject tobacco products to regulation under the FDCA, demonstrates that Congress intended to withhold such authority from the FDA. Having resolved the jurisdictional question against the agency, the Court of Appeals did not address whether the regulations exceed the FDA's authority under 21 U. S. C. § 360j(e) or violate the First Amendment.

We granted the federal parties' petition for certiorari, to determine whether the FDA has authority under the FDCA to regulate tobacco products as customarily marketed.

Claims of Therapeutic or Medical Benefit Are Absent

The FDA's assertion of jurisdiction to regulate tobacco products is founded on its conclusions that nicotine is a "drug" and that cigarettes and smokeless tobacco are "drug delivery devices." Again, the FDA found that tobacco products are "intended" to deliver the pharmacological effects of satisfying addiction, stimulation and tranquilization, and weight control because those effects are foreseeable to any reasonable manufacturer, consumers use tobacco products to obtain those effects, and tobacco manufacturers have designed their products to produce those effects. As an initial matter, respondents take issue with the FDA's reading of "intended," arguing that it is a term of art that refers exclusively to claims made by the manufacturer or vendor about the product. That is, a product is not a drug or device under the FDCA unless the manufacturer or vendor makes some express claim concerning the product's therapeutic benefits. We need not resolve this question, however, because assuming, *arguendo*, that a product can be "intended to affect the structure or any function of the body" absent claims of therapeutic or medical

Cigarettes Are Not Food or Consumer Drugs

The FDA [Food and Drug Administration] has only the powers that Congress has authorized. In 1938, as part of the New Deal, Congress created the FDA to regulate food and consumer drugs—prescription drugs, over-the-counter drugs, and even vitamins. Subsequently, Congress has granted the FDA authority to regulate cosmetics and medical devices such as pacemakers.

But cigarettes are not food. They are not over-the-counter or prescription drugs. They are not vaccines, medical devices, dietary supplements, cosmetics, medicines, or any other kind of consumer product that Congress has authorized the FDA to regulate.

Antitobacco officials in the FDA, however, pointed out that there was a drug in cigarettes—nicotine. Sure enough, nicotine is addictive, but it is not a medicine or dietary supplement. Nor is it an illegal drug, and if it were it would fall under the jurisdiction of the Drug Enforcement Agency and law enforcement.

Timothy P. Carney, The Big Ripoff: How Big Business and Big Government Steal Your Money. *Hoboken, NJ: John Wiley & Sons, 2006.*

benefit, the FDA's claim to jurisdiction contravenes the clear intent of Congress.

A threshold issue is the appropriate framework for analyzing the FDA's assertion of authority to regulate tobacco products. Because this case involves an administrative agency's construction of a statute that it administers, our analysis is governed by *Chevron U.S.A. Inc. v. Natural Resources Defense Council, Inc.* Under *Chevron,* a reviewing court must first ask "whether Congress has directly spoken to the precise question at issue." If Congress has done so, the inquiry is at an end; the court "must give effect to the unambiguously expressed intent of Congress."

But if Congress has not specifically addressed the question, a reviewing court must respect the agency's construction of the statute so long as it is permissible. Such deference is justified because "[t]he responsibilities for assessing the wisdom of such policy choices and resolving the struggle between competing views of the public interest are not judicial ones," and because of the agency's greater familiarity with the ever-changing facts and circumstances surrounding the subjects regulated.

In determining whether Congress has specifically addressed the question at issue, a reviewing court should not confine itself to examining a particular statutory provision in isolation. The meaning—or ambiguity—of certain words or phrases may only become evident when placed in context. . . . In addition, we must be guided to a degree by common sense as to the manner in which Congress is likely to delegate a policy decision of such economic and political magnitude to an administrative agency.

With these principles in mind, we find that Congress has directly spoken to the issue here and precluded the FDA's jurisdiction to regulate tobacco products.

Tobacco Products Are Not "Devices" Under the FDCA

Viewing the FDCA as a whole, it is evident that one of the Act's core objectives is to ensure that any product regulated by the FDA is "safe" and "effective" for its intended use. This essential purpose pervades the FDCA. For instance, 21 U. S. C. § 393(b)(2) defines the FDA's "[m]ission" to include "protect[ing] the public health by ensuring that . . . drugs are safe and effective" and that "there is reasonable assurance of the safety and effectiveness of devices intended for human use." The FDCA requires premarket approval of any new drug, with some limited exceptions, and states that the FDA "shall issue an order refusing to approve the application" of a new drug if it is not safe and effective for its intended purpose. If the FDA discovers after approval that a drug is unsafe or ineffective, it "shall, after due notice and opportunity for hearing to the applicant, withdraw approval" of the drug. The Act also requires the FDA to classify all devices into one of three categories. § 360c(b)(1). Regardless of which category the FDA chooses, there must be a "reasonable assurance of the safety and effectiveness of the device." Even the "restricted device" provision pursuant to which the FDA promulgated the regulations at issue here authorizes the agency to place conditions on the sale or distribution of a device specifically when "there cannot otherwise be reasonable assurance of its safety and effectiveness." Thus, the Act generally requires the FDA to prevent the marketing of any drug or device where the "potential for inflicting death or physical injury is not offset by the possibility of therapeutic benefit."

In its rulemaking proceeding, the FDA quite exhaustively documented that "tobacco products are unsafe," "dangerous," and "cause great pain and suffering from illness." It found that the consumption of tobacco products presents "extraordinary health risks," and that "tobacco use is the single leading cause of preventable death in the United States." It stated that "[m]ore than 400,000 people die each year from tobacco related illnesses, such as cancer, respiratory illnesses, and heart disease, often suffering long and painful deaths," and that "[t]obacco alone kills more people each year in the United States than acquired immunodeficiency syndrome (AIDS), car accidents, alcohol, homicides, illegal drugs, suicides, and fires, combined. Indeed, the FDA characterized smoking as "a pediatric disease," because "one out of every three young people who become regular smokers . . . will die prematurely as a result."

These findings logically imply that, if tobacco products were "devices" under the FDCA, the FDA would be required to remove them from the market. Consider, first, the FDCA's provisions concerning the misbranding of drugs or devices. The Act prohibits "[t]he introduction or delivery for introduction into interstate commerce of any food, drug, device, or cosmetic that is adulterated or misbranded." In light of the FDA's findings, two distinct FDCA provisions would render cigarettes and smokeless tobacco misbranded devices. First, § 352(j) deems a drug or device misbranded "[i]f it is dangerous to health when used in the dosage or manner, or with the frequency or duration prescribed, recommended, or suggested in the labeling thereof." The FDA's findings make clear that tobacco products are "dangerous to health" when used in the manner prescribed. Second, a drug or device is misbranded under the Act "[u]nless its labeling bears . . . adequate directions for use . . . in such manner and form, as are necessary for the protection of users," except where such directions are "not necessary for the protection of the public health." Given the FDA's conclusions concerning the health consequences of tobacco use, there are no directions that could adequately protect consumers. That is, there are no directions that could make tobacco products safe for obtaining their intended effects. Thus, were tobacco products within the FDA's jurisdiction, the Act would deem them misbranded devices that could not be introduced into interstate commerce. Contrary to the dissent's contention, the Act admits no remedial discretion once it is evident that the device is misbranded.

Second, the FDCA requires the FDA to place all devices that it regulates into one of three classifications. The agency relies on a device's classification in determining the degree of control and regulation necessary to ensure that there is "a reasonable assurance of safety and effectiveness." The FDA has yet to classify tobacco products. Instead, the regulations at issue here represent so-called "general controls," which the Act entitles the agency to impose in advance of classification. Although the FDCA prescribes no deadline for device classification, the FDA has stated that it will classify tobacco products "in a future rulemaking" as required by the Act. Given the FDA's findings regarding the health consequences of tobacco use, the agency would have to place cigarettes and smokeless tobacco in Class III because, even after the application of the Act's available controls, they would "presen[t] a potential unreasonable risk of illness or injury." As Class III devices, tobacco products would be subject to the

FDCA's premarket approval process. Under these provisions, the FDA would be prohibited from approving an application for premarket approval without "a showing of reasonable assurance that such device is safe under the conditions of use prescribed, recommended, or suggested in the proposed labeling thereof." In view of the FDA's conclusions regarding the health effects of tobacco use, the agency would have no basis for finding any such reasonable assurance of safety. Thus, once the FDA fulfilled its statutory obligation to classify tobacco products, it could not allow them to be marketed.

The FDCA's misbranding and device classification provisions therefore make evident that were the FDA to regulate cigarettes and smokeless tobacco, the Act would require the agency to ban them. In fact, based on these provisions, the FDA itself has previously taken the position that if tobacco products were within its jurisdiction, "they would have to be removed from the market because it would be impossible to prove they were safe for their intended us[e]." . . .

Contradicting Congressional Policy

Congress, however, has foreclosed the removal of tobacco products from the market. A provision of the United States Code currently in force states that "[t]he marketing of tobacco constitutes one of the greatest basic industries of the United States with ramifying activities which directly affect interstate and foreign commerce at every point, and stable conditions therein are necessary to the general welfare." More importantly, Congress has directly addressed the problem of tobacco and health through legislation on six occasions since 1965. . . . Nonetheless, Congress stopped well short of ordering a ban. Instead, it has generally regulated the labeling and advertisement of tobacco products, expressly providing that it is the policy of Congress that "commerce and the national economy may be . . . protected to the maximum extent consistent with" consumers "be[ing] adequately informed about any adverse health effects." Congress' decisions to regulate labeling and advertising and to adopt the express policy of protecting "commerce and the national economy . . . to the maximum extent" reveal its intent that tobacco products remain on the market. Indeed, the collective premise of these statutes is that cigarettes and smokeless tobacco will continue to be sold in the United States. A ban of tobacco products by the FDA would therefore plainly contradict congressional policy.

Viewpoint 3

> "In order to limit teenagers' access to cigarettes, we need to find a way to get them out of their social networks."

Raising the Minimum Age to Purchase Tobacco to Twenty-One Would Be Beneficial

Laurence Steinberg

In the following viewpoint, Laurence Steinberg proposes that raising the minimum age to purchase tobacco from eighteen to twenty-one would deter teen smoking. Antismoking education may have realistically accomplished what it can, Steinberg states, and warnings of tobacco addiction may inadvertently make smoking more attractive to teens. Raising the minimum age to purchase tobacco, however, would limit minors' access to cigarettes, as most get them from their peers, the author claims. He further cites a study reporting that raising the minimum age would reduce smoking among high school students to less than 10 percent in seven years. Steinberg is the Distinguished University Professor and Laura H. Carnell Professor of Psychology at Temple University.

The steady decline in teen smoking has stalled.

According to "Monitoring the Future," the University of Michigan's annual survey of the nation's adolescents, in 2006,

Laurence Steinberg, "Raise Age to Buy Cigarettes to 21," CNN.com, April 18, 2011.

about one-fifth of U.S. high school seniors smoked at least monthly, down from more than a third who did so in 1996. But in the past few years, that figure has not continued its steady drop.

The decline in regular smoking among younger students has similarly slowed, with rates at about 7% for eighth-graders and 14% for 10th-graders. Indeed, signs in the most recent surveys indicate that smoking among younger teenagers might be on the rise.

No one knows why rates of teen smoking haven't continued to fall, or what to do to get them to start dropping again. Virtually all American students still receive some sort of anti-smoking education, and there has been no weakening in restrictions on tobacco advertising.

The cost of cigarettes, usually a strong predictor of a decline in teen smoking, continues to rise. Yet more than 40% of today's high school students have tried smoking before they graduate, according to the Centers for Disease Control and Prevention.

Perhaps anti-smoking education has done about as much as it can be realistically expected to accomplish. We should not discontinue it, of course. But we need some other strategies. At the top of the list should be raising the minimum legal age for purchasing tobacco to 21.

Preventing Teen Smoking Is Critical

Smoking is by far the leading preventable cause of death in the United States. Because almost every adult smoker began smoking during adolescence, preventing teenagers from trying cigarettes is critical.

There now is solid evidence that smoking during early and mid-adolescence is far more likely to lead to addiction than is the same degree of smoking after age 21. (Animal studies similarly find that exposure to nicotine shortly after puberty is more addicting than exposure once adult maturity has been reached.) This is because the brain systems that are active when we experience pleasure are highly malleable during adolescence, and far

After an ongoing legal battle, the US Food and Drug Administration decided in 2013 to no longer pursue a proposed requirement for all tobacco companies to display graphic warning labels on cigarette packaging. © Steve Hamblin/Alamy.

more easily modified—sometimes permanently—by exposure to all sorts of drugs.

After 21, the same brain systems are much harder to change, which is good news for those who haven't tried smoking, drinking, or illicit drugs, but bad news for those who by that age are already hooked.

Some public health experts have called for graphic pictorial warnings on cigarette packs—pictures of diseased lungs, people having heart attacks, corpses, and the like—and late last year [in 2010] the FDA [Food and Drug Administration] unveiled the warning labels it will require beginning in 2012.

A few studies in countries where such warnings are already required have found that these labels may help motivate adult smokers who already want to quit. But there is no evidence that they will prevent teenagers from taking up the habit, and there are many reasons to think that they will not work. American

ALMOST ONE IN FOUR HIGH SCHOOL SENIORS SMOKES

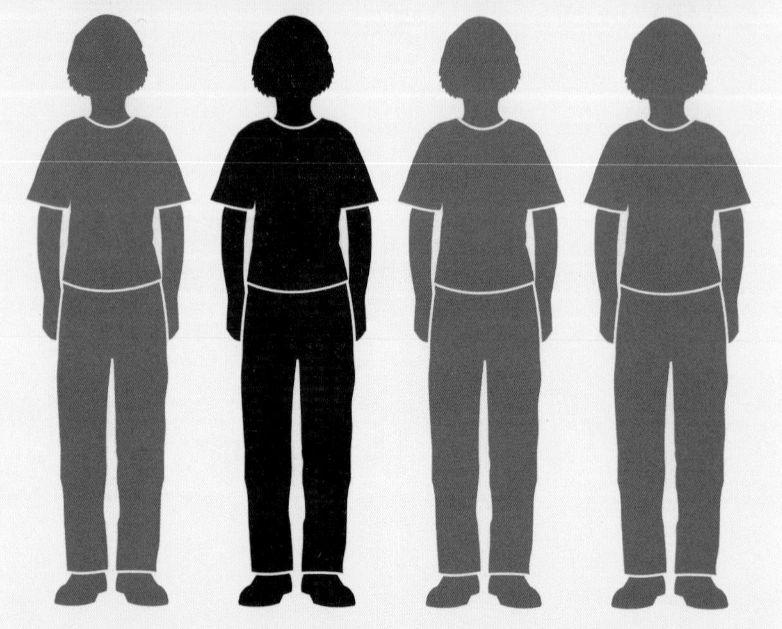

Taken from: US Surgeon General, *Preventing Tobacco Use Among Youth and Young Adults: A Report of the Surgeon General, 2012*. www.surgeongeneral.gov.

teenagers well understand the risks of smoking and know that it has harmful long-term health consequences.

The problem is that many adolescents believe that it is possible to smoke occasionally without becoming addicted—yet more than a third of individuals who start smoking as teenagers become daily smokers by the time they turn 18.

Reminding adolescents that cigarette smoking is potentially addictive, as some of the pictorial warnings will do, sounds like a good idea, but at least one study of adolescents' understanding of addiction cautions that telling them that smoking can be addictive may make cigarettes more, not less, attractive. When teenagers hear that something is addictive, they take that as an indication that it must be enormously pleasurable.

Raise the Purchase Age to Twenty-One

An alternative strategy to educating adolescents about the risks of smoking is limiting their access to cigarettes. This is an enormous challenge, though, because many adolescents who smoke don't get their cigarettes from retail outlets. They get them by bumming them from their friends. In order to limit teenagers' access to cigarettes, we need to find a way to get them out of their social networks.

The surest way to accomplish this is by raising the minimum legal purchase age for tobacco to 21. Currently, most states set this age at 18. (A small handful, as well as a few counties in New York, set it at 19.) The problem with the current arrangement is that it virtually guarantees that cigarettes will make their way into the hands of younger teenagers, with whom 18-year-olds regularly socialize.

Restricting sales of cigarettes to individuals 21 and older will both limit their legal sale to individuals who are less likely to become addicted, and will keep more cigarettes out of the hands of younger individuals who are far more vulnerable. According to one estimate, raising the purchase age to 21 would cut the proportion of high school students who smoke to less than 10% within seven years.

That, indeed, would be a breath of fresh air.

Viewpoint 4

"Studies show that effectively enforcing laws against cigarette sales to kids through regular compliance checks and penalizing retailers that sell to kids can significantly reduce youth smoking."

Enforcing Laws Prohibiting Cigarette Sales to Minors Prevents Youth Smoking

Jessica Guilfoyle

In the following viewpoint, Jessica Guilfoyle claims that effective enforcement of laws prohibiting the sale of tobacco to minors is necessary to reduce and deter underage smoking. Guilfoyle suggests that cigarettes remain easy for kids to buy, but routine compliance checks and penalties for retailers are proven to cut youth access to tobacco products. However, she alleges that voluntary programs established by cigarette companies are ineffective and never function properly. Guilfoyle offers the following recommendations for enforcement programs: adequate funding, no preempting of local ordinances, and educating retailers and the public. Guilfoyle is a research associate at Campaign for Tobacco-Free Kids in Washington, DC.

Strictly enforcing laws prohibiting tobacco sales to minors reduces youth smoking and is an important component of any comprehensive tobacco prevention campaign. While every state forbids retail sales to minors, these restrictions are often not enforced. Failing to enforce minimum-age laws not only wastes a constructive opportunity to reduce youth smoking but also tells kids that the laws need not be taken seriously—which undermines other tobacco-reduction efforts in the media, schools, and communities. The new federal FDA [Food and Drug Administration] tobacco law, however, makes selling cigarettes to youth a federal violation for the first time (as of June 22, 2010) and establishes a strong federal-state system for stopping sales to kids.

It's Too Easy for Kids to Buy Cigarettes

Each year, kids smoke more than 800 million packs of cigarettes, resulting in almost half a billion dollars in cigarette company profits—and the vast majority of these cigarettes are illegally sold to kids. Despite improvements in state efforts to stop retailer sales of tobacco products to youth, 14 percent of all 9th to 12th graders who smoke *usually* buy their cigarettes directly from a store, and others do so less frequently. Of the sales to youth smokers, nearly half (48.5%) of them were not asked to show proof of age when purchasing cigarettes. Not surprisingly, 58 percent of 8th graders and 80 percent of 10th graders say that cigarettes are fairly or very easy to get.

Efforts to reduce illegal cigarette sales to kids can have a direct impact on roughly three-quarters or more of all cigarettes smoked by kids. Besides those youth who buy directly, about 25 percent of kids report that they usually give money to other kids or adults to buy for them, and a third or more usually borrow their cigarettes from others (typically from kids who buy them directly). In addition, the heaviest and most regular youth smokers are the most likely to buy cigarettes directly from stores, and to supply cigarettes to other youths.

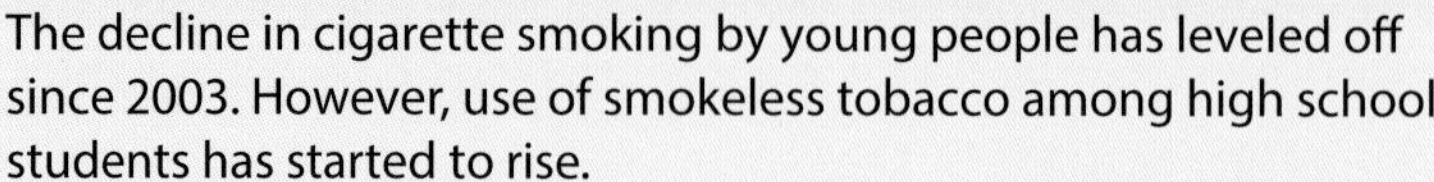

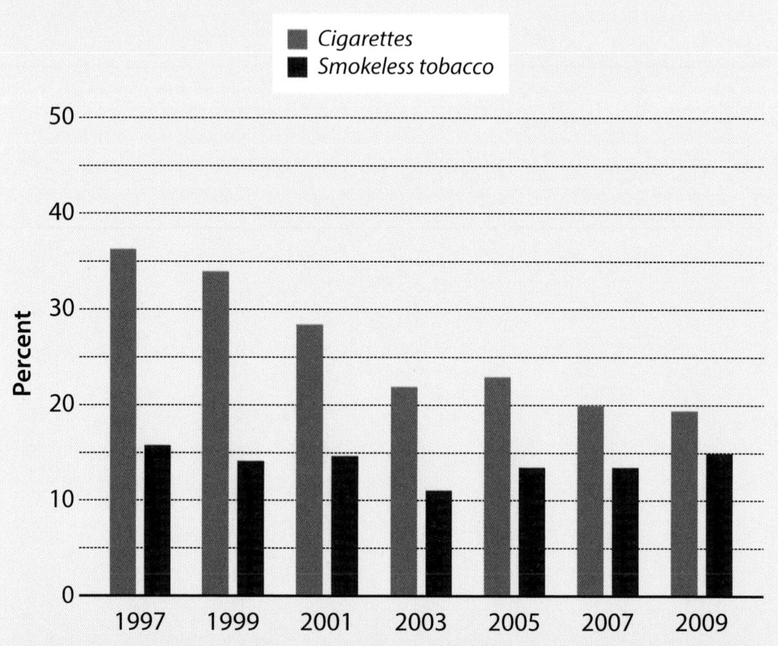

Taken from: Janet Loehrke, "Teen Tobacco 'Epidemic' Shocks Surgeon General," *USA Today*, March 8, 2012. usatoday.com.

Enforcement of Youth Access Laws Reduces Tobacco Sales to Minors

Studies show that effectively enforcing laws against cigarette sales to kids through regular compliance checks and penalizing retailers that sell to kids can significantly reduce youth smoking. In contrast, voluntary retailer compliance programs, such as those promoted by the big cigarette companies, do not.

- A study published in the *Annals of Family Medicine* found that youth who perceived cigarettes as relatively easy to get were more likely to become regular smokers than those who perceived cigarettes as more difficult to obtain.

- A Canadian study examining tobacco retailers surrounding schools found that retailer density is linked to youth access. It concluded that selective enforcement of youth access laws in retail outlets close to schools may help prevent underage youth from smoking.
- A study done in Chicago in 2006 found that tobacco retailers were disproportionately located in areas with lower social and economic levels. It also found that youths in areas with a higher density of tobacco retailers were 13 percent more likely to have smoked in the past month than youths living in areas with lower tobacco retail density. This suggests that reductions in retail tobacco outlet density may reduce rates of youth smoking.
- A 2004 study conducted in California contrasted youth manipulative behavior with retailer behavior in contributing to underage tobacco sales. The results showed that retailer behavior was the strongest predictor of cigarettes sales to youth and reiterated the need for intervention with retailers.
- By analyzing FDA compliance checks across the country, a 2003 study found that state polices significantly affect the sale of tobacco products to minors. Stores located in states with fewer/weaker compliance policy measures were 36 percent more likely to illegally sell tobacco to minors than stores located in states with more effective measures.
- A study of 14 Minnesota communities in the *American Journal of Public Health* showed that an intervention involving local ordinances and enforcement to limit youth access to tobacco significantly reduced adolescent smoking rates.
- A 1997 study analyzing youth access policies, compliance, and enforcement concluded that aggressive and comprehensive approaches to limiting youth access will lead to significant reductions in youth smoking.

Many argue that restrictions on tobacco sales to minors are often not properly enforced, sending the negative message to teenagers that smoking is not a big deal. © Alain Le Bot/Getty Images.

- A *Journal of American Medical Association* study found that a comprehensive youth access program in Woodridge, Illinois, reduced sales to minors from 70 percent to less than 5 percent in a year and a half, while reducing tobacco use among youth by over 50 percent.
- Comprehensive tobacco prevention programs in California and Massachusetts that included strong enforcement of youth access laws substantially reduced illegal sales to mi-

nors. In California, the proportion of retailers who failed compliance checks for selling tobacco products to minors decreased from 52 percent in 1994 to 21.7 percent in 1997. In Massachusetts, illegal retailer sales dropped from 48 to eight percent. After Massachusetts slashed its tobacco control funding and sharply curtailed its periodic retailer compliance checks, however, the average rate of illegal sales to minors in that state more than tripled.

Voluntary Cigarette Company Programs Do Not Work

To block the rigorous enforcement of effective federal, state, or local laws to prevent illegal sales of tobacco products to youth, the tobacco industry regularly claims that its own voluntary "anti-youth-access" programs will adequately protect against such sales to kids. But those voluntary programs are inherently flawed, have never been implemented effectively, and have never functioned properly to reduce youth access to tobacco products or stop illegal cigarette sales to kids. For example, one study found that tobacco product retail stores with "We Card" signs had average youth sales rates roughly equal to those stores with no signs at all, and were significantly more likely to make illegal sales to minors than those retail outlets with government-sponsored signs about no tobacco product sales to youths.

Key Elements of an Enforcement Program

Based on solid research findings, state attorneys general and other experts have recommended that any effort to reduce youth access to tobacco products include the following key elements:

- Designating an agency with clear responsibility for enforcement
- Providing adequate, guaranteed funding for enforcement

- Making frequent and realistic compliance checks, with a goal of sustained 95 percent compliance
- Meaningful penalties including graduated fines and ultimately, prohibiting sales of tobacco products
- No preemption of local ordinances
- Education and awareness efforts for merchants and the public.

5

Viewpoint

"*Smoking is for the young.*"

Teens Should Be Able to Smoke

N. Stephan Kinsella

In the following viewpoint, N. Stephan Kinsella insists that teens should be allowed to smoke. The argument that children do not possess the maturity or judgment to assess the inherent risks of smoking is flawed, he claims. Rather, the long-term effects of tobacco use drop dramatically after quitting, Kinsella suggests, and teens can end the habit early with virtually no health consequences. Also, he rejects the argument that selling cigarettes to children violates the wishes of parents and declares that they—not tobacco companies or retailers—are responsible for preventing youths from smoking. A legal libertarian theorist, the author is a patent attorney, founder of the Center for the Study of Innovative Freedom, and former adjunct professor at South Texas College of Law.

Libertarians quite properly believe the tobacco companies should be free to sell cigarettes to consumers, without fear of liability. The smoker chooses to take the risk of smoking, and

N. Stephan Kinsella, "Let Kids Smoke," LewRockwell.com, July 25, 2000.

Some argue that teens should be legally allowed to smoke, and youth smoking does not pose a serious long-term health threat. © Caroline Purser/Getty Images.

he has a right to do so. Yet even libertarians seem to accept the notion that cigarettes should not be sold to minors. In the tradition of libertarian critical inquiry, I have a one question for them: why? Why restrict the liberty of R.J. Reynolds & Co. to sell to kids? After all, other vendors sell kids candy and cokes, CDs and movie tickets. Presumably the little crumb crunchers have enough legal capacity to form a contract to purchase at least some consumer items. Why not tobacco?

Kids are generally not allowed to engage in harmful or dangerous activities (such as parachuting, rock-climbing) or to take actions with permanent consequences (such as getting a tattoo, having a child) without parental consent. The child's consent alone is not enough. The argument seems to be that cigarettes, too, are harmful or have permanent consequences. Thus the child is not yet competent to choose to permanently harm himself by smoking. The tobacco companies have been browbeaten into repeating this line. R.J. Reynolds states on its website that it "does not want children to smoke, not only because it is illegal to sell to minors in every state, but also because of the inherent health risks of smoking and because children lack the maturity of judgment to assess those risks."

But this argument is flawed. Even if we assume that smoking can increase the risk of disease, it is widely known that quitting smoking greatly reduces smoking-related risks. After all, as anti-smoking fanatics routinely say, *It is never too late to stop smoking*. They maintain, for example, that by quitting smoking you will live longer and have a lower chance of having a heart attack or cancer. Anti-smoking zealots and other assorted health nuts never quite come right out and say that if you quit smoking early enough, you eventually get back to normal. Yet, some do admit that, at least for heart disease, "About 15 years after quitting the risk is close to that of persons who have never smoked." And they acknowledge that the sooner you quit, the better.

Youthful Smoking Does Not Pose a Serious Long-Term Health Threat

But all this means that youthful smoking, by itself, does not pose a serious long-term health threat. Take a boy who starts smoking at age 15. When he turns 18, he has already been smoking for three years. At that point, he is mature enough to stop smoking, if he wants. Surely, if he never smokes again, the effects of three youthful years of smoking will wane as the years go by. It does not seem plausible that a few years of smoking in his teens will appreciably increase long-term health risks.

On the other hand, as an adult, he can now decide to continue smoking, despite the risks of doing so. This continued smoking may indeed lead to detrimental health consequences down the road, if it continues long enough. But any long-term

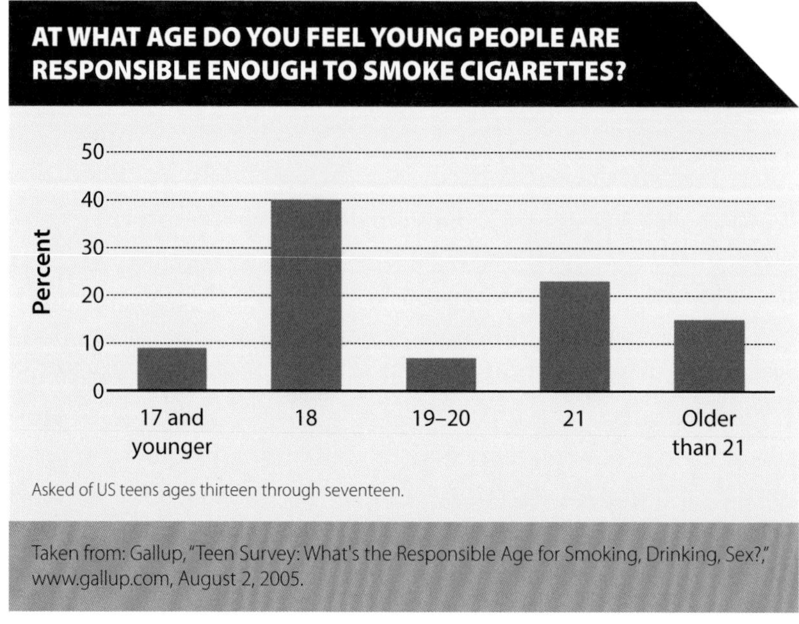

harm incurred will be due to his decisions, as an adult, to continue smoking. It will not be because of a few years of youthful fun. Thus, the kid's smoking does not pose a long-term danger to his health. Only continued smoking after he turns 18 does—but such a decision is within the adult's rights.

But wait, it could be argued, the problem in this theory is that tobacco (nicotine) is addictive. The newly minted smoking adult cannot simply choose to quit smoking, because of the addiction inflicted on this body when he was a minor. Thus, because tobacco is addictive, the kid is inflicting a long-term, permanent harm on himself, which a child is not competent to do.

Addiction Is a Myth

Rubbish. Addiction is a myth. It is incompatible with free will. The 18-year-old clearly has a choice to continue smoking or not. The fact that his body is chemically addicted to nicotine simply means that there is a cost incurred—withdrawal symptoms, and the like—if he chooses to quit smoking. But all choices have opportunity costs, and the choice to stop smoking is no different than any other in this regard.

What about the argument that parents have the right to prohibit their kids from smoking, and most parents do oppose their kids smoking, and thus selling to kids presumptively is done in violation of the parent's wishes? Some parents do permit their kids to make purchases, if not for their own use, then for the use of adults—e.g., Dad sends Junior down to the 7-11 to pick up a pack of Marlboro Lights. Why should this sale be prohibited? As for kids who buy and smoke cigarettes against their parents' wishes—it is the parents' job to discipline their kids, not tobacco companies or convenience stores. Forcing Junior to smoke a whole pack of cigarettes until he's blue in the face; or making him eat two or three cigarettes, as a boyhood friend of mine experienced, ought to be sufficient to put the fear of God in him for a while.

So I say, let's bring back the Joe Camel mascot—and recruit Barney, Mickey Mouse, and Pokemon while we're at it. Smoking is undeniably cool. Let people enjoy it when they can. Smoking is for the young.

VIEWPOINT 6

"If teens and young adults see tobacco use in their homes or in public places within their communities, these images encourage them to see smoking as a normal part of adult behavior."

Numerous Factors Influence Teens to Smoke

Centers for Disease Control and Prevention

In the following viewpoint, the Centers for Disease Control and Prevention (CDC) states that a variety of factors encourage and enable teen smoking. It points out that adolescents are more physically vulnerable to forming an addiction to nicotine than adults. Social and environmental influences portray smoking as a cool and edgy behavior, continues the CDC, and seeing tobacco use in their homes, communities, and entertainment sends the message to teens that it is normal. Moreover, suggests the CDC, the tobacco industry uses tactics to make their products affordable, accessible, and appealing to the age group through retail marketing, packaging, and media advertising. A part of the US Department of Health and Human Services, the CDC conducts and supports public health activities.

Tobacco use by teens and young adults remains shockingly high in the United States. Today, more than 3.6 million mid-

Preventing Tobacco Use Among Youth and Young Adults, www.cdc.gov, 2012, pp. 2–3, 8–12.

dle and high school students smoke cigarettes. In fact, for every person who dies due to smoking—more than 1,200 each day—at least two youth or young adults become regular smokers. Nearly 90% of these replacement smokers try their first cigarette by age 18. Clearly, we have not solved the problem.

Examining the Statistics

Today's teens and young adults can access information on millions of subjects almost instantly. But many of the same media that warn of the dangers of tobacco use also carry messages that smoking is cool—edgy—adult. That's one reason nearly 4,000 kids under age 18 try their first cigarette every day. That's almost 1.5 million youth a year.

In fact, nearly 9 out of 10 smokers start smoking by age 18, and 99% start by age 26. On any given day, more than 2,500 youth and young adults who have been occasional smokers will become regular smokers. And at least a third of these replacement smokers will die early from smoking.

The percentage of youth who smoke went down every year between 1997 and 2003.

But since then, the decrease in teen smoking has slowed and the use of some forms of tobacco by youth has leveled out. Today, one out of four high school seniors and one out of three young adults under age 26 are smokers. . . .

Why Young People Use Tobacco

There are many reasons young people begin using tobacco. Teenagers, and even preteens, are developing behaviors, social connections, and attitudes. They often experiment with different behaviors because they see these behaviors in peers they admire, in adults they hope to be like someday, or in media or entertainment idols.

Social Influences Adolescents and young adults are very susceptible to social influences. If they see tobacco use as a normal behavior because their friends or family members use tobacco, young people are more likely to try tobacco themselves.

Teens and young adults highly value their friendships and want to fit in with their group. What their peers do—and especially what the leaders of their social groups do—can have a strong influence on what they do. Young people whose friends smoke are much more likely to smoke as well.

Physical Influences Nicotine is just as addictive as heroin and cocaine. Because they are sensitive to nicotine, teens can feel dependent on tobacco sooner than adults. There is also evidence that genetics might make it more difficult for some young people to quit smoking once they have started.

Environmental Influences Teens and young adults are sensitive to what they see and hear in the world around them. If they are exposed to images that portray smokers as cool, attractive, rebellious, fun-loving, risk-taking, or other characteristics they admire, young people may want to smoke, too. Such images are often found in advertising displays at convenience stores and other outlets that sell tobacco. Communities that allow the sale of cigarettes and other tobacco products near schools have higher rates of youth tobacco use than do communities that have tobacco-free zones around schools. If teens and young adults see tobacco use in their homes or in public places within their communities, these images encourage them to see smoking as a normal part of adult behavior.

Movies For many years, tobacco companies paid studios to have their products appear in movies. Even though this practice is no longer allowed, movies for youth, and even some movies for children, may include images of characters using tobacco. These images are powerful because they can make smoking seem like a normal, acceptable, or even attractive activity. Young people may also look up to movie stars, both on and off screen, and may want to imitate behaviors they see.

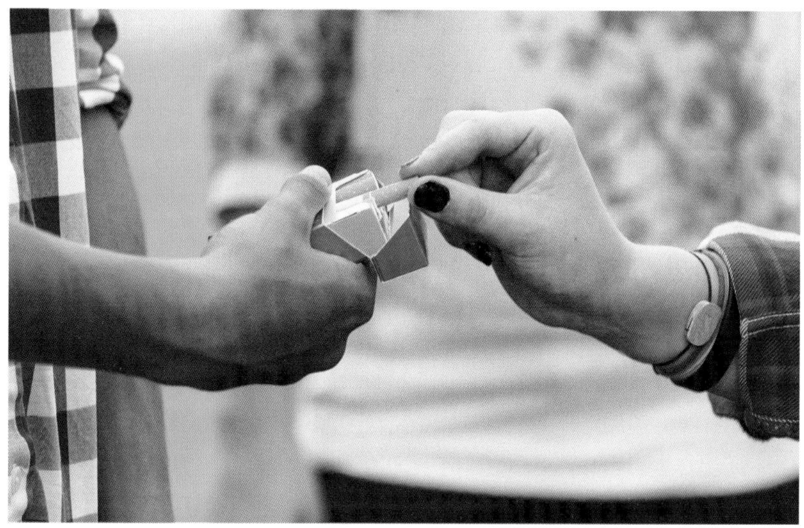

More than 3.6 million middle and high school students smoke cigarettes. Peer pressure is one of many factors that contribute to teen smoking. © MachineHeadz/Getty Images.

Over time, the number of images of tobacco use in movies has gone down. But movies still contain thousands of images of tobacco use that are proven to encourage young people to start smoking. In 2010, nearly a third of top-grossing youth-rated movies—those with G, PG, or PG-13 ratings—contained images of tobacco use.

How the Tobacco Industry Targets Young Consumers

Tobacco companies use multiple methods and spend lots of money to convince young people that using tobacco is OK—even attractive. Their business depends on getting these young consumers to try—and to keep using—their products. Young people are responsive to marketing, making them vulnerable to messages that encourage tobacco use.

Keeping Prices Down Tobacco companies lower prices through coupons and other promotions so that consumers can afford to buy their products. Teens are especially sensitive to pricing.

In 2008, cigarette makers spent nearly $10 billion to market their products. Much of this spending—$6 out of every $7—was used to pay for price cuts through coupons, sales, and giveaways. Similarly, smokeless tobacco makers spent about $3 out of every $4 of their $547 million marketing budget to keep prices low.

Making Products Easy to Buy A number of laws limit face-to-face and vending machine sales of tobacco products to young people. But there is less oversight online. While most websites say buyers must be at least 18 years old, research found that 15- and 16-year-olds were able to place orders successfully. Nearly 8 out of 10 of those young people received their orders, and only 1 out of 10 shipments required proof of age at the time of delivery of the tobacco product.

Designing Products That Appeal To Youth Cigarettes that appeal to new smokers are often smoother and milder to improve taste and reduce the body's physical reaction to the smoke. While flavored cigarettes are now prohibited, the industry still puts fruit flavoring and other kid-friendly flavors in many of their cigars. This is especially true for cigarette-sized cigars, which are now available in many flavor varieties—such as grape and strawberry—that youth find appealing in other products. Many of these little cigars look exactly like cigarettes with a darker wrapper.

Many smokeless products are also flavored. These include chew and snuff—which come in a variety of forms—and new smokeless products, such as dissolvable tobacco. All of these products can cause serious health problems and lead to nicotine addiction and future smoking. And tobacco companies are still using different techniques to make many cigarette brands taste less harsh—especially brands that young people often use when they start smoking.

Young people sometimes use smokeless tobacco products in places where cigarettes are banned, such as schools. Snus (dry

Movies: A Model for Smoking

People are not the only source of a model for smoking; movies can be a source of social pressure. Movies aimed at adolescent audiences contain more positive messages about cigarette smoking than R-rated movies. A growing body of evidence implicates movies as a source of influence to begin smoking. [Researcher] John Pierce and his colleagues have examined the influence that movies have on young adolescents and have found that they are highly influenced by viewing their favorite movie stars smoking on film. In a series of studies, Pierce and his colleagues asked adolescents to list their favorite movie star. Next, they reviewed popular films to count the number of times favorite stars smoked on film. The researchers found that viewing a popular movie star smoking on screen created a powerful incentive for girls to begin smoking, but the influence was not as strong for boys.

Linda Brannon and Jess Feist, Health Psychology: An Introduction to Behavior and Health. *Belmont, CA: Wadsworth, 2010.*

snuff in a pouch), and dissolvable smokeless products in particular, provide a discreet way for young people to maintain their addiction to nicotine even when they can't smoke. In fact, most youth users of these smokeless products also smoke cigarettes. The biggest danger of these products is that they may introduce kids to nicotine, putting them at risk for nicotine addiction.

Creating a Package That Appeals to Youth

Packaging has a powerful visual impact. Users come to associate certain brands with certain qualities. Words on packages, such as "slims" and "thins," push the myth of weight loss. Before they were banned, some words ("low tar," "light," "mild") falsely suggested safety. Studies show that color makes a difference too. Smokers tend to think that cigarettes in lighter-colored packs are "lighter" and safer than cigarettes in darker-colored packs—even when both packs contain the exact same cigarettes.

Retail Marketing Tobacco companies use many marketing and advertising tools at stores that sell tobacco products. Even the locations where tobacco products are sold can have an impact on tobacco use by young people. For example, more cigarettes are sold in convenience stores than in any other type of store, and 70% of adolescents shop in convenience stores at least once a week—where they are more likely to be exposed to prosmoking messages.

For many years, the tobacco industry has offered sellers financial rewards and discounts when they sell large volumes of their products. Some stores and gas stations place tobacco products on or near checkout counters—a visible spot that may trigger impulse buying.

They also run sales on tobacco products and place vivid, eye-catching ads in windows and outside their buildings. Ads inside the store are sometimes at eye level for preteen children, which research shows might influence them to try tobacco products later.

Using Media to Promote Products

The tobacco industry uses media to promote its products to young people. Here are some of the channels it uses.

Digital Media Many cigarette companies use websites to promote their products. Some of these websites feature videos, games, coupons, and contests that may appeal to youth. Meanwhile, some young people are using social networking channels (Facebook, Twitter, discussion forums, message boards, and YouTube videos) to sing the praises of tobacco, especially to their peers.

Magazines Tobacco ads are not allowed on TV or on billboards. But they may still be found in mainstream magazines targeted to adults, and many young people read these. These ads often suggest that using tobacco can make you sexy, popular, thin, and cool.

"[Smoking] just seems to be, like picking up guitar or growing your hair out, just another way to try to be cool, which as teenagers, is something we all struggle with."

A Teen Discusses Why She Thinks Her Peers Smoke

Personal Narrative

Andrea Domanick

In the following viewpoint, Andrea Domanick discusses the possible reasons her peers smoke. For instance, Domanick asserts that popular culture and society frequently associate cigarettes with maturity and rebelliousness, influencing some of her friends to pick up the habit. As for her personal stance against tobacco, Domanick credits her involvement with an antismoking movement but admits that she accepts the decision of others to light up. Additionally, the author asserts that innovative and effective strategies to prevent teen smoking have been replaced by uninspiring campaigns and, despite its risks, the behavior is still viewed as a way to be cool. At the time of publication, Domanick was a student at Harvard-Westlake School in the Los Angeles area.

The crowd cheers. "Thank you!" yells Maja Ivarson, lead singer of the Swedish band The Sounds. The tall blonde struts across the stage in tight leather pants and takes a moment to light a cigarette from the guitarist.

"If ya don't smoke, you should! It makes ya look cool," she shouts as the next song starts up. She's mocking herself, since the band chain-smokes throughout the set, but as my friends and I dance and yell, I can't help but think, damn, she's right.

Though I don't smoke, what she said got me wondering. Yeah, cigarettes are just awful for you, but honestly, there's something about their attractive, rebellious image that emanates "cool."

Why Do Teens Start Smoking?

Despite all the information out there about the risks of smoking (such as cancer, heart disease and impotence) I've noticed an increase in smoking in youth and pop culture, particularly in the art and music scenes. So while the numbers may be going down nationally (according to a 2003 survey, down 6 percent from 1997), smoking seems more and more popular among my friends and other teens I encounter. More and more of my friends' blog pictures are of them posing with cigarettes. Though I can't think of a valid reason to smoke, I wonder why others do. Is it really just for the glamour, or is there something else that compels teens to turn a blind eye to large warning labels on their cigarette packs?

"I began smoking because I was hanging with a really intellectual crowd when I was in 11th grade, all of whom smoked," said 18-year-old Brian Lehrer, a former student from my school, Harvard-Westlake, who now attends the University of British Columbia in Canada. "Smokers are a community that thrives particularly on generosity and intellectualism."

I first noticed a connection between smoking and pop culture when I began subscribing to *Rolling Stone* a few years ago. To my dismay, brightly colored cigarette ads paraded their way across several pages in each issue. It also seemed that nearly every photograph that wanted to convey a sense of maturity or rebelliousness featured a smoking celebrity—from [actor] Johnny

Depp to skinny-tie bands like Interpol to even the look-who's-all-grown-up [actor] Macaulay Culkin.

I see how some of my friends got sucked in.

Accepting Others' Decision to Smoke

Smoking certainly isn't something I condone, but I don't impose my feelings about it on others. I respect their choice, and they respect mine. Usually they're just as aware of its risks as I am. Several friends have even admitted to wanting to stop.

"Initially, I really enjoyed smoking because I like to feel like a rebel," Brian said. "[But] what I initially used to assert power over my parents and exude an appearance of coolness has ironically caused me to inadvertently portray myself as vulnerable and unattractive."

© O'Farrell, The Illawarra Mercury, Australia/Cagle Cartoons.

Bingo. All tolerance aside, I can't help but wonder how a cancer-causing addiction that gives a good portion of your self-control and money to one of the largest and most evil corporations in America portrays an against-the-grain image? You just look like a sexy, cool . . . pawn of corporate America?

I largely credit my stance on smoking to the provocative messages of the Truth campaigns from when I was younger. I was even on the street team, posting informative stickers on telephone poles and wearing their shirts to school, despite the smirks of my classmates.

Today's Antismoking Campaigns Aren't Effective

Over the years, my views have stayed the same, but the Truth shirts haven't left my drawers. It was easy for me in seventh grade to campaign against Big Tobacco; no one I knew smoked yet. However, as friends took up the habit, I learned that it was as important to accept their decision to smoke as it was for them to accept my decision not to. "Bad habit" does not necessarily equal "bad person"—all putting down a smoker will do is make them less open-minded to quitting and isolate you from a potential new friendship or more.

And while I don't say anything when my friends light up, I feel like today's anti-smoking campaigns are wimpy. I no longer see billboards with images of cowboys smoking limp cigarettes or the guerrilla-style Truth ads, with team members doing things like surrounding Big Tobacco headquarters with body bags for each smoking death in the past year. Instead they seem to be getting replaced by three generations of a family gleefully crowded around a computer screen that reads "Ways to Quit Smoking! From your friends at Procter & Gamble." That's about as inspiring as an OxiClean commercial.

But despite all the campaigning, a 2003 survey by the Centers for Disease Control and Prevention reported that 21.9 percent of high school students still smoke.

Monte Wilson, 17, a friend from Santa Cruz who recently quit smoking says, "[I started smoking] because I wanted to be cool. There is honestly no other reason to do it. Any benefits [like those from smoking] can be obtained from something that doesn't kill you. . . . Gradually I enjoyed [smoking] more and more, but never really that much."

Oddly enough, I found myself tempted to smoke this summer. When I went to study creative writing at a program called InnerSpark in Valencia everyone smoked. We regularly walked to a nearby strip mall and had the 18-year-olds get cigarettes for everyone from the smoke shop. My friends teased me because I "chain-chewed" bubble gum to resist smoking—it was hard! While I was there, I even developed a certain affection for cigarettes; over the month I learned the brands and smells of the different kinds my friends smoked. But the last thing I wanted to be was a hypocrite, so I never tried one.

Most of my friends at InnerSpark admitted to intending to quit. "I'll quit before I'm 30," and "I'll quit when I get pregnant," were common refrains.

I was hoping when I started writing this piece that I would uncover some secret legit reason that people smoke. But it just seems to be, like picking up guitar or growing your hair out, just another way to try to be cool, which as teenagers, is something we all struggle with. But unlike a bad haircut, it's important to realize smoking is a habit that puts something much greater than your social life at risk.

Viewpoint 8

"[Tobacco companies] know that marketing their cigarettes to youth is essential to each company's success and longevity, and for that reason create marketing campaigns designed to increase youth consumption."

Tobacco Advertising Has Targeted Youths

The US District Court's Decision

Gladys Kessler

In 1999, the US Department of Justice sued numerous tobacco companies for racketeering by deceiving consumers of the harmful health effects and addictive quality of cigarettes. Years later, in United States v. Philip Morris *(2006), the US District Court for the District of Columbia found the companies guilty of violating the Racketeer Influenced and Corrupt Organizations Act and engaging in widespread fraud. In the following viewpoint, Senior Judge Gladys Kessler claims that tobacco advertising has directly targeted youths. Disputing the argument that the ads are intended to persuade smokers to switch brands, Kessler asserts that the companies recruit young consumers because they are most likely to smoke—and form brand loyalties—for life. She continues that cigarette marketing is proven as a contributing factor in initiating smoking among youths, bombarding them with positive imagery of tobacco. Kessler has served the court since 1994 and assumed office in 2007.*

Gladys Kessler, *United States v. Philip Morris*, US Court District Court for the District of Columbia, August 17, 2006.

Every year, over 400,000 people die of smoking-related diseases. In addition, there are a relatively small number of people who quit smoking each year. In order to sustain and perpetuate themselves, Defendants must bring in new smokers to replace those leaving the market. Each cigarette manufacturing company gains a small amount (less than 10%) of smokers through "switching" or changing brands. Only about 9% of adult smokers switch among Defendants' brands. Defendants' own employees admit that brand switching rates are low and falling. According to David Beran, Executive Vice President of Strategy, Communications and Consumer Contact for Philip Morris, the brand switching rate for 1997 was 4.0%, was 6.3% for 2002, and was 5.4% for 2003. Switching, by definition, does not bring in new smokers to the industry as a whole.

The only way Defendants can sustain themselves is by bringing in large numbers of replacement smokers each year. Carl Schoenbachler, current president and CEO [chief executive officer] of BATIC (a former parent of B&W Tobacco and holding entity for B&W Tobacco) acknowledged that although the company has a stated policy of not marketing to non-smokers, "it was a reasonable conclusion" that B&W would become unprofitable if non-smokers did not become smokers.

The majority of people who become addicted smokers start smoking before the age of eighteen, and many more before the age of twenty-one. Ellen Merlo, Senior Vice President at Philip Morris, admitted that she was aware that over 80% of smokers start smoking before they turn eighteen. A 1989 RJR [R.J. Reynolds Tobacco Company] document titled "Camel Y&R Orientation" discussed the "strategic importance" of young adult smokers ("YAS"): "YAS are the only source of replacement smokers. Less than one-third of smokers start after age 18." The document further stated: "To stabilize RJR's share of total smokers, it must raise share among 18–20 from 13.8% to 40% . . . ASAP." In a September 20, 1982, memorandum, Diane S. Burrows, RJR Marketing Development Department researcher, stated, "if a man has never smoked by age 18, the odds are three-to-one he never will. By age 21, the odds are twenty-to-one."

Moreover, smokers are remarkably brand-loyal. Defendants realize that they need to get people smoking their brands as young as possible in order to secure them as lifelong loyal smokers. As Bennett LeBow, President of Vector Holdings Group, stated, "if the tobacco companies really stopped marketing to children, the tobacco companies would be out of business in 25 to 30 years because they will not have enough customers to stay in business."

Youth Are Crucial to the Tobacco Industry

In internal documents, Defendants admit that stimulating youth smoking initiation and retaining and increasing their share of the youth market is crucial to the success of their businesses. For example, in a 1999 slide presentation, titled "ASU30 [Adult Smoker Under 30] Project," manager Rick Stevens analyzed BATCo's "ASU30 Performance 1998," stating that younger adult smokers were a "critical factor in the growth and decline of every major brand and company over the last 50 years." Furthermore, a slide, titled "Value of YAS," recognized that "[m]arket renewal is almost entirely from 18 year old smokers" and "[n]o more than 5% start smoking after age 24."

Defendants know that marketing their cigarettes to youth is essential to each company's success and longevity, and for that reason create marketing campaigns designed to increase youth consumption. As United States marketing expert Dr. Robert Dolan explained:

> The trend in tobacco companies' spending on marketing has continued to increase dramatically. Tobacco industry spending of $2 billion on advertising and promotion in 1980 reached $4 billion in 1988 and then $6 billion in 1994. After four years around the $6 billion mark, spending shot up [to] $11.2 billion by 2001. In 2002, the last year for which data is available,

> the tobacco companies spent $12.47 billion, an increase of 11.61% over 2001. The fundamental dynamic of the industry has not changed though. The tobacco companies knew that brand loyalty is a key phenomenon and if someone doesn't start smoking as a teenager, he or she is unlikely to start. . . . Defendants still represent that the only objective of marketing is impacting brand choice while they implement marketing programs which increase the value potential customers see in smoking—attracting people including teenagers to the market and deterring others from quitting.

In a February 29, 1984, memorandum, titled "Younger Adult Smokers: Strategies and Opportunities," to Martin Orlowsky, CEO of Lorillard, Diane Burrows, market researcher at R.J. Reynolds, stated:

> Younger adult smokers have been the critical factor in the growth and decline of every major brand and company over the last 50 years. They will continue to be just as important to brands/companies in the future for two simple reasons. . . .

The renewal of the market stems almost entirely from 18 year old smokers. No more than 5% of smokers start after age 24. The brand loyalty of 18-year-old smokers far outweighs any tendency to switch with age. . . . Marlboro and Newport, the only true younger adult growth brands in the market, have no need for switching gains. All of their volume growth can be traced to younger adult smokers and the movement of the 18-year-olds which they have previously attracted into older age brackets, where they pay a consumption dividend of up to 30%. A strategy which appealed to older smokers would not pay this dividend. . . . Younger adult smokers are the only source of replacement smokers. Repeated government studies. . . . have shown that: Less than one-third of smokers (31 %) start after age 18. . . . Thus, today's younger adult smoking behavior will largely determine the trend of Industry volume over the next several decades. If younger adults turn away from smoking, the Industry must decline, just as a population which does not give birth will eventually dwindle.

In an April 13, 1984, RJR letter, R.C. Nordine stated that "[i]t is relatively easy for a brand to retain eighteen-year-old smokers once it has attracted them. . . . Conversely, it is very difficult to attract a smoker that has already been won over by a different brand."

Targeting Young Adult Smokers Is a Key Corporate Priority

A March 1988 report, titled "Younger Adult Smoker Opportunity," discussed "RJR's most critical strategic need—Younger Adult Smokers." The report stated: "Improved younger adult development is a key Corporate priority . . .—Necessary for core brand revitalization (#1 Corporate priority)—Lack of younger adults responsible for total Company volume trend." It indicated that RJR's "marketing department [was] refocusing efforts against younger adult smokers." The report indicated the importance of unrestricted advertising for reaching these younger smokers and stated that a possible advertising ban "would severely limit RJR's ability to introduce [a] new brand or attract younger adult smokers." The report also stated that "[y]ounger adult smokers drive the growth of two major competitors"—Marlboro and Newport—which were "capturing an ever increasing share of younger adult smokers." Finally, the report explained that young smokers were crucial to the continuing survival of RJR because teenagers remain loyal to their brand of choice as they age and because teenagers smoke an increasing volume of cigarettes as they become adults: "[Y]ounger adult smokers are the key to future growth for any company or brand for several reasons: (1) Aging explains 75% of SOM [Share of Market] growth. (2) Benefits of younger adult smokers compound over time as a result of brand loyalty and the increase in rate per day as smokers age." In summary, the report stated, "RJR must begin now to capture younger adult smokers:—Volume decline inevitable without

YAS—Potential for future advertising restrictions—Marketing department restructured to address the issue."

Marketing reports prepared for RJR, under the heading "Decision to Smoke," included the following statement: "66% of all new smokers by age 18." The document also reported on the brand loyalty of smokers, indicating that "90% [of] smokers use only one brand," and that the "Implications for 90's" are that eighteen to twenty-four year olds will be "[c]ritical to long term brand vitality as consumption increases with age." Another report prepared for RJR, from approximately 1989, titled "Younger Adult Smokers," discussed the strategic importance of younger adult smokers, stating that "YAS are the only source of replacement smokers—[l]ess than one-third of smokers start after age 18." The report analyzed the differences between "FUBYAS" [First Usual Brand Young Adult Smokers] (ages 18 to 20) and "Switchers" (ages 21 to 24), stating that "FUBYAS are in transition—belonging to the FAMILY (secure) replaced by belonging to selected PEER GROUP (not as secure)."

In a letter dated October 12, 1989, titled "Dollar Value of YAS Over Time," Burrows provided "estimates . . . of the value of capturing Younger Adult Smokers and holding them over time." The letter calculated the profits that RJR would gain "[i]f an 18 year old adopts an RJR full price brand" for 3 years ($1,359), for 7 years ($3,710), for 10 years ($6,148), or for over 20 years ($18,794). Burrows concluded:

> Our aggressive Plan calls for gains of about 5.5 share points of smokers 18–20 per year, 1990–93 (about 120,000 smokers per year). Achieving this goal would produce an incremental cash contribution of only about $442MM during the Plan period (excluding promotion response in other age groups and other side benefits). However, if we hold these YAS for the market average of 7 years, they would be worth over $2.1 billion in aggregate incremental profit. I certainly agree with you that this payout should be worth a decent sized investment.

Increasing the Number of Young Adult Smokers

An RJR document, titled "1990 Workplan Objectives," stated that "[t]he number one priority for 1990 is to obtain younger adult smoker trial and grow younger adult smoker share of market."

The Joe Camel character, as seen on this 1994 Camel cigarette billboard, came under harsh criticism for appealing directly to youth consumers. A 1998 study found that the top three cigarette brands bought by underage smokers were also the three most heavily advertised brands. © Richard Levine/Alamy.

In addition, the document asked "Why target the YAS market?" and answered:

> Each Year:
>
> 800,000 new smokers (18+) enter the market
>
> 1,500,000 smokers leave the market
>
> With about 50 million smokers, this means that each year there are:
>
> 1.6 share points of new smokers
> 3.0 share points of quitters
>
> At least 95% of all new smokers are 18–24. About 70% are exactly 18 (i.e., aged in the 18+ market).

Each brand and company has a share of new smokers and quitters, which is reflected in their shares of YAS and older smokers. These shares drive long-term market performance.

Carl Schoenbachler, current president and CEO of BATIC (a former parent of B&W [Brown & Williamson] Tobacco and holding entity for B&W Tobacco), when asked if the statement, "The key to sustainable long-term profit growth in the U.S. is ASU 30," was accurate, responded: "Yes, I would say that's true." He explained that:

> there tends to be a great deal of loyalty in cigarette brands. So, just a natural mathematical equation would suggest if you—if you don't have thirty-year-olds smoking your product, you won't have forty-year-olds and fifty-year-olds. It's a very brand loyal business.

Defendants' Marketing Is a Substantial Contributing Factor to Youth Smoking Initiation

Cigarette marketing, which includes both advertising and promotion, is designed to play a key role in the process of recruiting young, new smokers by exposing young people to massive amounts of imagery associating positive qualities with cigarette smoking. Research in psychology and cognitive neuroscience demonstrates how powerful such imagery can be, particularly for young people, in suppressing perception of risk and encouraging behavior. Defendants' own statistics demonstrate how successful they have been in marketing their three main youth brands: Philip Morris's Marlboro, RJR's Camel, and Lorillard's Newport.

The Complex Link Between Marketing and Youth Smoking

In 1989, the Surgeon General concluded:

> There is no scientifically rigorous study available to the public that provides a definitive answer to the basic question of whether advertising and promotion increase the level of tobacco consumption. Given the complexity of the issue, none is likely to be forthcoming in the foreseeable future.

In her 1994 Report, Youth and Tobacco: Preventing Tobacco Use Among Young People, the Surgeon General [Joycelyn Elders] echoed these sentiments and further warned that the debate "about whether tobacco promotion 'causes' young people to smoke" was "misguided because single-source causation is probably too simple an explanation for any social phenomenon."

Social scientists are increasingly uncomfortable applying the term "causation" and its corresponding rigorous criteria, which require proof of consistency, strength, specificity, temporality, and coherence of the association, in describing social behavioral phenomena. Government expert Dr. Dean Krugman noted he would "never phrase the question [of the relationship between marketing and youth smoking initiation] in a causal manner":

> You cannot look at advertising and promotion and get a direct causal link to behavior. That has been well cited in the literature, it's been well cited in the 1994 Surgeon General's Report, that the whole notion of positing a causal question is really not

germane to understanding if there is influence between advertising and sales promotion and youth behavior.

Marketing Is a Substantial Contributing Factor to Youth Smoking Initiation

In her 1994 Report, the Surgeon General pointed out:

> A substantial and growing body of scientific literature has reported on young people's awareness of, and attitudes about, cigarette advertising and promotional activities. Research has also focused on the effects of these activities on the psychosocial risk factors for beginning to smoke. Considered together, these studies offer a compelling argument for the mediated relationship of cigarette advertising and adolescent smoking.

In the same Report, the Surgeon General explicitly addressed and rejected Defendants' claims that their marketing activities are directed only toward adult brand-switchers:

> Even though the tobacco industry asserts that the sole purpose of advertising and promotional activities is to maintain and potentially increase market shares of adult consumers, it appears that some young people are recruited to smoking by brand advertising. Two sources of epidemiologic data support the Surgeon General's assertion. Adolescents consistently smoke the most advertised brands of cigarettes. . . . Moreover, following the introduction of advertisements that appeal to young people, the prevalence of the use of those brands—or even the prevalence of smoking altogether—increases.

The Surgeon General further noted in the 1994 Report:

> Current research suggests that pervasive tobacco promotion has two major effects: it creates the perception that more people smoke than actually do, and it provides a conduit between actual self-image and ideal self-image—in other words, smok-

ing is made to look cool. Whether causal or not, these effects foster the uptake of smoking, initiating for many a dismal and relentless chain of events.

In the 1998 Surgeon General's Report, *Tobacco Use Among U.S. Racial/Ethnic Minority Groups,* the Surgeon General concluded that:

> Advertising is an important influence on tobacco use initiation and maintenance. . . . Cigarette advertising and promotion may stimulate cigarette consumption by . . . encouraging children and adolescents to experiment with and initiate regular use of cigarettes. . . . In addition, cigarette advertising appears to influence the perceptions of youths and adults about the pervasiveness of cigarette smoking and the images they hold of smokers.

This 1998 Report also pointed out that:

> Available data indicate that young people smoke the brands that are most heavily advertised. In 1993, the three most heavily advertised brands of cigarettes, Marlboro, Camel, and Newport, were the most commonly purchased brands among adolescent smokers.

In the 2000 Surgeon General's Report, *Reducing Tobacco Use,* the Surgeon General stated that:

> [i]ntensive review of the available data . . . suggests a positive correlation between level of advertising and overall tobacco consumption—that is, as advertising funds increase, the amount of tobacco products purchased by consumers also increases.

Moreover,

> [i]ndirect evidence of the importance of advertising and promotion to the tobacco industry is provided by surveys that

PERCENTAGE OF STUDENTS WHO PREFER MARLBORO, CAMEL, AND NEWPORT CIGARETTES

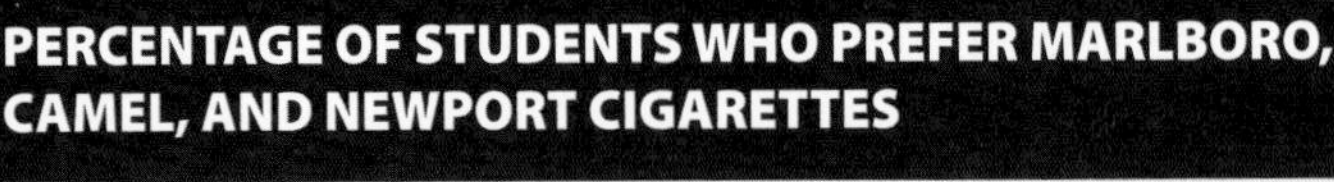

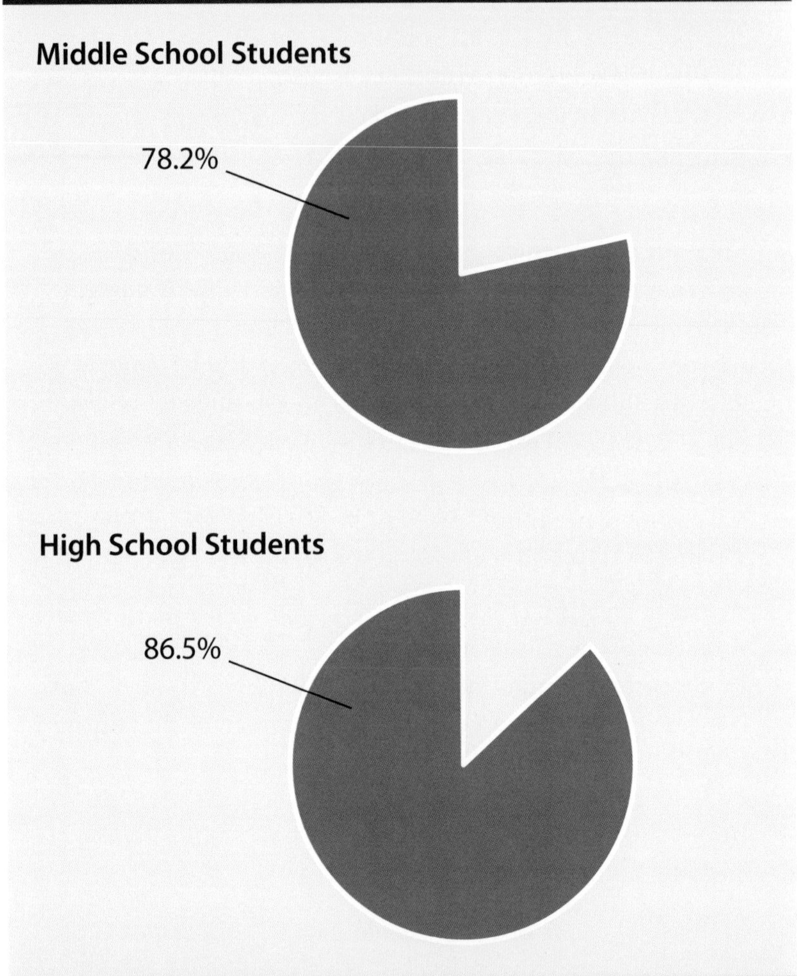
Middle School Students
78.2%
High School Students
86.5%

Taken from: Centers for Disease Control and Prevention, *Morbidity and Mortality Weekly Report*, vol. 58, no. 5, February 13, 2009.

suggest that most adolescents can recall certain tobacco advertisements, logos, or brand insignia; these surveys correlate such recall with smoking intent, initiation, or level of consumption.

Advertising and Promotion Recruit New Smokers

In her 2000 Report the Surgeon General rejected Defendants' claims that their main purpose in advertising is to maintain brand loyalty and increase market share among current smokers and found that "[c]onsiderable evidence" supported the hypothesis that "advertising and promotion recruit new smokers." The Surgeon General stated:

> Attempts to regulate advertising and promotion of tobacco products were initiated in the United States almost immediately after the appearance of the 1964 report to the Surgeon General on the health consequences of smoking. Underlying these attempts is the hypothesis that advertising and promotion recruit new smokers and retain current ones, thereby perpetuating a great risk to public health. The tobacco industry asserts that the purpose of marketing is to maintain brand loyalty. Considerable evidence has accumulated showing that advertising and promotion are perhaps the main motivators for adopting and maintaining tobacco use.

Regarding the Joe Camel campaign, the Surgeon General noted in the 2000 Report:

> The role of advertising is perhaps best epitomized by R.J. Reynolds Tobacco Company's Camel brand campaign (initiated in 1988) using the cartoon character 'Joe Camel.' Considerable research has demonstrated the appeal of this character to young people and the influence that the advertising campaign had on minors' understanding of tobacco use and on their decision to smoke.

Moreover,

> an increase in smoking initiation among adolescents during 1985–1989 has been ecologically associated with considerable

> increases in promotion expenditures [by the tobacco industry], as exemplified by the Joe Camel campaign.

The 1992 United Kingdom Department of Health, Economics and Operational Research Division publication, "The Effect of Tobacco Advertising on Tobacco Consumption: A Discussion Document Reviewing the Evidence," concluded that:

> the great majority of the results [of aggregate statistical studies] point in the same direction—towards positive impact [on tobacco consumption]. The balance of evidence thus supports the conclusion that advertising does have a positive impact on consumption.

The Department of Health further concluded, regarding studies of advertising bans in other countries, that "[i]n each case the banning of advertising was followed by a fall in smoking on a scale which cannot reasonably be attributed to other factors [other than the advertising ban]."

Tobacco Advertising Is Particularly Attractive to Adolescents

The Institute of Medicine, chartered in 1970 by the National Academy of Sciences, which advises the Federal government on science, engineering and Medicare and enlists distinguished members of the appropriate professions in the examination of policy matters pertaining to the health of the public, earlier reached a similar conclusion. The 1994 Institute of Medicine publication "Growing Up Tobacco Free, Preventing Nicotine Addiction in Children and Youths" concluded:

> The images typically associated with advertising and promotion convey the message that tobacco use is a desirable, socially approved, safe and healthful, and widely practiced behavior among adults, whom children and young people want to emulate. As a result, tobacco advertising and promotion

> undoubtedly contribute to multiple and convergent psychological influences that lead children and youths to begin using these products and to become addicted to them.

Other reputable experts have concurred with the conclusions drawn by the Surgeon General. NCI's Monograph 14: Changing Adolescent Smoking Prevalence, a 2001 National Cancer Institute publication, found:

> Tobacco advertising and promotional activities are an important catalyst in the smoking initiation process. A review of the existing evidence on the relationship between exposure to advertising or having a tobacco promotional item and smoking behavior . . . suggests that there is a causal relationship between tobacco marketing and smoking initiation.

Regarding the numerous studies which examine the role of tobacco advertising and promotion in smoking initiation, NCI's Monograph 14 concluded that:

> When [these studies are] viewed as a group . . . the conclusion that there is a causal relationship between tobacco marketing and smoking initiation seems unassailable. . . . [T]obacco advertisements are particularly attractive to adolescents who, for one reason or another, are looking for an identity that the images are carefully designed to offer.

> *"In light of the history of past industry practices, industry messages targeted at children and adolescents should be regarded as presumptively suspect."*

Targeting Youths by Tobacco Companies Should Be Banned

Richard J. Bonnie, Kathleen Stratton, and Robert B. Wallace

In the following viewpoint, Richard J. Bonnie, Kathleen Stratton, and Robert B. Wallace assert that strategies tobacco companies use to target youths under the age of eighteen should be banned, including antismoking programs. Bonnie, Stratton, and Wallace allege that many of the programs were not designed to prevent youth smoking but to deter regulation and gain access to the youth market. For instance, the industry sought to build credibility and give their programs legitimacy by partnering with youth organizations, the authors contend, as well as collecting data about minors through prevention campaigns. Therefore, they recommend that tobacco companies only be allowed to carry out prevention efforts through independent nonprofit organizations. Bonnie was

Richard J. Bonnie, Kathleen Stratton, and Robert B. Wallace, *Ending the Tobacco Problem: A Blueprint for the Nation Committee on Reducing Tobacco Use*. National Academies Press, 2007, pp. 327–330. Courtesy of the National Academies Press, Washington, DC.

chair, Wallace was vice chair, and Stratton was study director of the Committee on Reducing Tobacco Use: Strategies, Barriers, and Consequences. The authors also edited Ending the Tobacco Problem: A Blueprint for the Nation.

For more than two decades, tobacco companies have promoted youth smoking education and prevention programs. Early efforts, introduced in the mid-1980s, were aimed at both children and parents; sample themes included "Talk to Your Kids," "Kids Don't Smoke," "Smoking Isn't Cool," and "Wait Until You're Older." The youth programs portrayed smoking as an adult activity that was inappropriate for teenagers, whereas the parent-oriented messages urged adults to be involved in their children's decision making regarding smoking.

Fending Off Regulation and Deflecting Public Scrutiny

Despite touting these programs as being designed to discourage teenagers from smoking, internal industry documents now reveal that, from their inception, these campaigns were developed largely to fend off increased regulation and to deflect public scrutiny of industry marketing practices. Industry representatives hoped that their youth prevention programs (which ignored the health effects of smoking) would displace the educational initiatives developed by public health groups, which frequently presented smoking as distasteful and unhealthy.

In the early 1990s, tobacco companies shifted their youth smoking prevention efforts to retailers, launching promotional efforts that included messages such as "It's the Law," "We Card," and "Support the Law." These campaigns implied that, in addition to age, upholding the law was an important reason not to smoke; moreover, the programs served to shift attention away from the industry's contributions to youth smoking. Through these youth smoking prevention programs, the industry was able to recruit a network of retailers to assist it in detecting and defeating local tobacco control legislation, such as youth-access measures, advertising restrictions, and clear-indoor-air laws. The industry also used the presence of this retailer network to fight national legislation, arguing that FDA [Food and Drug Administration] regulation of tobacco advertising was unnecessary because the We Card program was making a "measurable difference".

By the late 1990s, the tobacco companies sought the assistance of third parties to disseminate youth smoking prevention messages. By building alliances with youth organizations such as 4-H and Boys and Girls Clubs, tobacco companies sought to gain credibility with the public and create an aura of legitimacy for their prevention efforts. Industry documents reveal that the companies expended very little (if any) effort to study the effect of their campaigns on reducing the rate of smoking among youth; yet, the industry carefully assessed the public relations outcomes associated with the third-party programs.

Industry documents also reveal that the youth smoking prevention campaigns also enabled the companies to obtain useful data about the teen market that was otherwise practically inaccessible to them through standard marketing surveys. For example, the Philip Morris company learned that a smoking prevention advertisement directed at young teens would likely receive little attention from older youth if the message were delivered by members of the younger age group. Thus the company chose not to target teens in the 15- to 18-year-old age group—those at the highest risk for smoking—with their prevention campaigns. The Lorillard company developed a similarly innovative approach, inviting teenagers to visit the company's website to learn more about its youth smoking prevention campaign. When these individuals enter personal information to qualify for sweepstakes, the company also obtains potentially useful data about the youth market.

A company's efforts to disseminate informational materials about its programs may constitute no more than veiled attempts to promote its corporate identity among children. The California

Reviewing the Tobacco Industry's Messages

- Who is communicating and why?
- Who owns, profits from, and pays for the message?
- How is the message communicated (ex: Philip Morris black- and-white TV ad)?
- Who receives the message? What do they think they mean?
- What is the intended purpose of the message? Whose point of view is behind the message?
- What is NOT being said and why?
- Is the message consistent within itself? Is it part of a coherent message strategy or does it stand out in some way?

Florida Tobacco Control Clearinghouse, "The Truth About Big Tobacco's Counteradvertising Campaign," 2012. www.cimes.fsu.edu.

Departments of Education and Justice confronted such an attempt by Philip Morris in 2000, when the company distributed book covers promoting its youth prevention campaign to schools in California. This fairly blatant commercial ploy aroused opposition among educators statewide who argued that Philip Morris could have supported existing programs proven to be effective if it had been sincerely interested in helping to reduce the rate of smoking among youth.

A Skeptical View of the Industry's Motivation

Within the last decade, tobacco companies have expanded youth smoking prevention programs worldwide and have increased their financial commitments to these programs. Philip Morris

The warning sign "We Card" is part of a youth-directed antismoking campaign funded by tobacco companies. Skeptics believe that these campaigns are a tactic by tobacco companies to distract focus away from their contributions to youth smoking though advertising and other methods. © Richard Levine/Alamy.

announced a $100 million "Think. Don't Smoke." campaign in 1998, and provided more than $125 million in grants to schools and youth organizations to support youth smoking prevention, youth development, and youth smoking cessation programs between 1999 and 2004. Similarly, Lorillard has contributed more than $80 million to youth smoking prevention programs since 1999. As in the United States, international campaigns have frequently sent messages that have focused on decision making rather than on the negative health effects of smoking and that have presented smoking as an adult activity.

When these expenditures are viewed in terms most favorable to the companies, these expenditures are designed to demonstrate good corporate citizenship on the youth smoking issue and, perhaps, to weaken political support for stronger regulation. However, tobacco control advocates have a more skeptical view of the industry's motivation. According to tobacco control advocates, these "youth prevention" programs are not really designed to prevent youth smoking at all. Instead, they are designed to promote smoking by facilitating industry access to young people through marketing surveys, by counteracting the anti-industry message of tobacco control media efforts by portraying the industry as trustworthy, and finally, by beginning to establish brand identification for future smokers.

In the [National Academy of Sciences' Committee on Reducing Tobacco Use] view, it is not necessary to resolve this dispute regarding the industry's motivation. In light of the history of past industry practices, industry messages targeted at children and adolescents should be regarded as presumptively suspect. The only acceptable justification for an industry-sponsored youth-oriented program is to prevent youth smoking. However, there is no evidence that the industry's prevention programs actually do reduce youth smoking, and there is some evidence that they do not. If the tobacco manufacturers are genuinely interested in preventing youth from smoking, they should support programs known to be effective and should contract with an independent nonprofit organization with the necessary expertise to carry out the program. To the extent that the companies have a legitimate interest in demonstrating good corporate citizenship, this interest can be served by requiring the recipients of company funding to acknowledge company support for its activities.

> Recommendation: Congress and state legislatures should prohibit tobacco companies from targeting youth under 18 for any purpose, including dissemination of messages about smoking (whether ostensibly to promote or discourage it) or to survey youth opinions, attitudes and behaviors of any kind. If a tobacco company wishes to support youth prevention programs, the company should contribute funds to an independent nonprofit organization with expertise in the prevention field. The independent organization should have exclusive responsibility for designing, executing and evaluating the program.

The Proposed Restriction and the Constitution

The constitutionality of the proposed restriction is not free from doubt, since it curtails the freedom of tobacco companies to communicate with young people for any purpose. However, the proposal does not ban all communication with minors, and the mere exposure of minors to advertising would not be a violation of the proposed ban. Instead, the restriction bans "targeting" of young people (conduct that is also banned by the MSA when it is explicitly promotional). The committee's proposal extends the MSA ban to all targeting of youth, based on the presumption that any communications that target young people are highly likely to reflect a promotional motivation. Any legislation seeking to implement this restriction could certainly allow room for a company to prove that a specific communication had a legitimate purpose and did not have the purpose or effect of promoting tobacco use. On the basis of this analysis and on the unique history of tobacco company efforts to promote youth smoking, the committee believes that the proposed restriction would survive a constitutional challenge.

VIEWPOINT 10

> *"The advertising restrictions . . . are not drawn narrowly to achieve the stated public purpose and, as such, fail to comply with the free speech protections of the First Amendment."*

Banning Tobacco Ads Infringes the Freedom of Speech

Caroline Fredrickson and Michael MacLeod-Ball

In the following viewpoint, Caroline Frederickson and Michael MacLeod-Ball contend that restrictions on tobacco ads to reduce youth smoking under the 2009 Family Smoking Prevention and Tobacco Control Act infringe upon the First Amendment. The restrictions are more limiting than necessary and not narrowly tailored to prevent teens from smoking, they state. Frederickson and MacLeod-Ball conclude that such regulations impose personal preferences on unpopular products. Caroline Fredrickson is director of the Washington legislative office of the American Civil Liberties Union (ACLU). Michael MacLeod-Ball is chief legislative and policy counsel for the ACLU.

We are writing on behalf of the American Civil Liberties Union (ACLU) to express our concern over the advertising

Caroline Fredrickson and Michael MacLeod-Ball, "ACLU Calls for Narrowing Advertising Restrictions in S.982, The Family Smoking Prevention and Tobacco Control Act," American Civil Liberties Union, June 1, 2009.

restrictions contained in S. 982, The Family Smoking Prevention and Tobacco Control Act (hereinafter the '2009 Tobacco Control Bill'). The ACLU is America's largest and oldest civil liberties organization, having over half a million members, countless additional activists and supporters, and 53 affiliates nationwide. We last commented on the issue of tobacco advertising regulation when S. 2626, the Youth Smoking Prevention and Public Health Protection Act of 2002 (hereinafter the '2002 Youth Smoking Bill'), was introduced during the 107th Congress. As in 2002, we continue to believe that the advertising restrictions in this year's [2009] bill are not drawn narrowly to achieve the stated public purpose and, as such, fail to comply with the free speech protections of the First Amendment. In the absence of a much more substantial narrowing of the advertising restrictions in a manner directly tied to the goal of reducing youth smoking, we urge the removal of the advertising restrictions set forth in Section 102 of the bill. It is our understanding that such an amendment is likely to be offered when the bill comes to the floor for consideration and we urge you to support it.

Regulating the Tobacco Industry

In 1995 the Food and Drug Administration (FDA) proposed regulations to restrict the sales and distribution of cigarettes and smokeless tobacco products to children and adolescents. In March of 2000, in *FDA v. Brown & Williamson Tobacco Corp.*, the Supreme Court ruled that Congress had not granted the FDA jurisdiction to regulate tobacco products as customarily marketed and the regulations were consequently revoked. The 2002 Youth Smoking Bill would have amended the Federal Food, Drug, and Cosmetic Act to give the Secretary of Health and Human Services (HHS) regulatory authority over tobacco products. In doing so the legislation would have codified the past restrictions (61 Fed. Reg. 44398, Aug. 28 1996). In the statement we submitted to the Senate Health, Education, Labor and Pensions Committee on September 18, 2002, we argued that:

1. The restrictions imposed by S. 2626 on advertising and other promotions of tobacco were inconsistent with the First Amendment; and
2. Restrictions on speech intended to reduce the number of children who begin smoking must be narrowly defined so as not to infringe on the rights of adults.

The 2009 Tobacco Control Bill would now impose most of the same restrictions as the 2002 Youth Smoking Bill. The only significant change impacting commercial speech restrictions is the acknowledgment of the ruling in *Lorillard Tobacco Co. v. Reilly* [2001]. In *Lorillard,* the Supreme Court struck down a state tobacco advertising regulation similar to the FDA's proposed rule. The Massachusetts regulation would have prohibited outdoor ads within 1,000 feet of schools, parks and playgrounds and also restricted point-of-sale advertising for tobacco products. Writing for the majority, Justice [Sandra Day] O'Connor found the Massachusetts regulation was not narrowly tailored

The 2009 Family Smoking Prevention and Tobacco Control Act prohibits tobacco companies from advertising on race cars. Some argue that bans on tobacco advertisements violate the US Constitution. © Darrell Ingham/Getty Images.

© Mike Luckovich/Cartoonist Group.

enough to meet constitutional scrutiny. She also suggested the FDA regulation faced the same problem.

Section (102)(2)(E) of the 2009 Tobacco Control Bill responds to the *Lorillard* ruling by requiring new regulations to:

> Include such modifications to section 897.30(b) [of 61Fed. Reg. 44615-44618], if any, that the Secretary determines are appropriate in light of governing First Amendment case law, including the decision of the Supreme Court of the United States in *Lorillard Tobacco Co. v. Reilly.*

Misuse of the Regulatory Process

While we agree this is a step in the right direction, there is no affirmative adjustment to the prohibited restriction and only an implicit acknowledgement of the First Amendment implications of the ruling. Moreover, the remaining restrictions were left largely intact and we do not believe they are any more narrowly tailored to the public purpose of reducing youth smoking than the outdoor ad restriction addressed in *Lorillard.* The remaining restrictions would, among other things:

1. Restrict all advertising to black and white format;
2. Allow unrestricted advertising in only those publications which have an 85% or more adult readership, and fewer than 2 million youth readers;
3. Restrict labeling and advertising in an audio format to words without music, and limit video format to static black text on a white background;
4. Ban logo and brand names on race cars, driver uniforms, and the like;
5. Ban the use of tobacco brand names on non-tobacco products (e.g. t-shirts, caps, lighters);
6. Ban the use of tobacco brand names associated with non-tobacco products;
7. Ban brand-name event sponsorships; and
8. Ban distribution of free product samples, either in person or through the mail.

Under First Amendment analysis, any such speech limitation must be no more restrictive than necessary and must directly advance the government's objective in reducing smoking by youths. In 2002, we noted that neither FDA studies nor legislative findings were sufficient to meet the *Liquormart* [*44 Liquormart v. Rhode Island* (1996)] test. Nothing in the 2009 record causes us to change our opinion in that regard. Regulating commercial speech for lawful products only because those products are widely disliked—even for cause—sets us on the path of regulating such speech for other products that may only be disfavored by a select few in a position to impose their personal preferences through misuse of the regulatory process. Instead, we suggest a determined application of the laws prohibiting false advertising and a continuation of the vigorous and successful efforts to warn the American public—including its children—of the harms associated with the use of tobacco products. Usually, the antidote to harmful speech can be found in the wisdom of countervailing speech—not in the outright ban of the speech perceived as harmful.

We urge you to support any amendment that would remove the advertising restrictions in Section 102 of S. 982.

"That the two laws provide different definitions of 'public place' does not by itself render the ordinance void."

Government-Mandated Bans and Ordinances Against Smoking Apply to All Public Places

The Missouri Court of Appeals' Decision

Thomas H. Newton

In City of Kansas City v. Carlson *(2009), the owner of a sports bar in Missouri was cited under a municipal ordinance for permitting smoking indoors. The owner argued that the ordinance conflicted with the state's Indoor Clean Air Act (ICAA), which does not define an establishment of the type and size of the sports bar as a public place. In the following viewpoint, excerpted from the Missouri Court of Appeals opinion, Judge Thomas H. Newton argues that the ICAA does not explicitly make smoking immune from regulation, but deems the bar as an unregulated area. The municipal ordinance does not conflict with the state law, but enlarges it, Newton maintains. Moreover, while the ICAA and ordinance define public spaces differently, he states, the restriction on smoking is still*

Thomas H. Newton, *City of Kansas City v. Carlson*, Missouri Court of Appeals, Western District, June 23, 2009.

effective. Newton is a judge for the Missouri Court of Appeals, Western District.

JC Sports Bar is a bar and billiard parlor in Kansas City that posts signs stating "Nonsmoking Areas are Unavailable." In June of 2008, Kansas City Ordinance No. 080073 went into effect. The ordinance prohibits smoking in enclosed public places and places of employment, with some exceptions for hotels and casinos. It also provides that "A person having control of a public place or place of employment and who fails to comply with the provisions of this Article shall be guilty of an ordinance violation[.]" In July of 2008, the Kansas City Health Department cited Ms. Carlson for allowing patrons to smoke in JC's.

In municipal court, Ms. [Georgia Jean] Carlson moved to dismiss the charge, contending that the ordinance conflicted with the ICAA [Indoor Clean Air Act] and was thus preempted. The municipal court found Ms. Carlson guilty and sentenced her to a fine of $100. Ms. Carlson appealed to the circuit court, which held a trial de novo on stipulated facts. Ms. Carlson again moved to dismiss the charge, contending that the ordinance conflicted with the ICAA. After hearing argument, the circuit court rejected Ms. Carlson's contention. It noted that the state legislature "could have but did not expressly provide that there could be no further regulation of smoking by any other authority" and was "not convinced that a definitional exclusion of certain businesses" was equivalent to preemption. It ordered Ms. Carlson to pay the $100 fine and court costs. Ms. Carlson appeals.

In a court-tried case we sustain the trial court's judgment unless there is no substantial evidence to support it, it is against the weight of the evidence, or it erroneously declares or applies the law. Because this case was tried on stipulated facts, the only question for our review is whether the trial court made the proper legal conclusions. Whether a city exceeds its statutory authority in passing an ordinance is an issue we review de novo [from the beginning].

Excluded Places Are Unregulated

In her sole point on appeal, Ms. Carlson argues that the City's ordinance irreconcilably conflicts with state law. She contends that because the ICAA excludes bars such as JC's from its definition of public places, it affirmatively permits smoking in JC's while Kansas City's ordinance prohibits it. The City, however, maintains that the ICAA does not "permit" smoking in bars and billiard parlors. Rather, it leaves those places unregulated, which creates no conflict with municipal regulation that enlarges on the state scheme.

Kansas City is organized under article VI, section 19 of the Missouri Constitution as a constitutional charter city.

Under section 19(a), the City has:

> all powers which the general assembly of the state of Missouri has authority to confer upon any city, provided such powers are consistent with the constitution of this state and are not limited or denied either by the charter so adopted or by statute. Such a city shall, in addition to its home rule powers, have all powers conferred by law.

Section 19(a) thus gives Kansas City "all the power which the legislature could grant," unless otherwise limited by the constitution, statutory law, or its charter.

This section of the Missouri Constitution was adopted in 1971. Prior to the amendment's adoption, Missouri courts sought specific authority for exercises of municipal power.... The intent behind amending section 19(a) was to "insure the supremacy of the legislature while at the same time putting only minimal and necessary limitations on the power of municipalities." Thus, "[u]nder Missouri's new model of home rule ... the municipality possesses all powers which are not limited or denied by the constitution, by statute, or by the charter itself."... *Yellow Freight Sys., Inc. v. Mayor's Comm'n on Human Rights*. Consequently, because the City's power is derived from amended section 19(a), the instant case requires us to ask not whether the City had authority

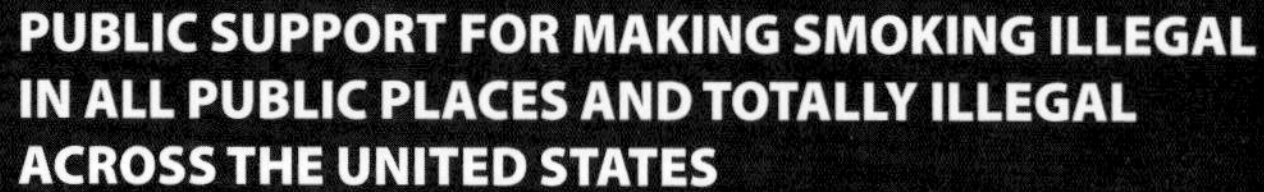

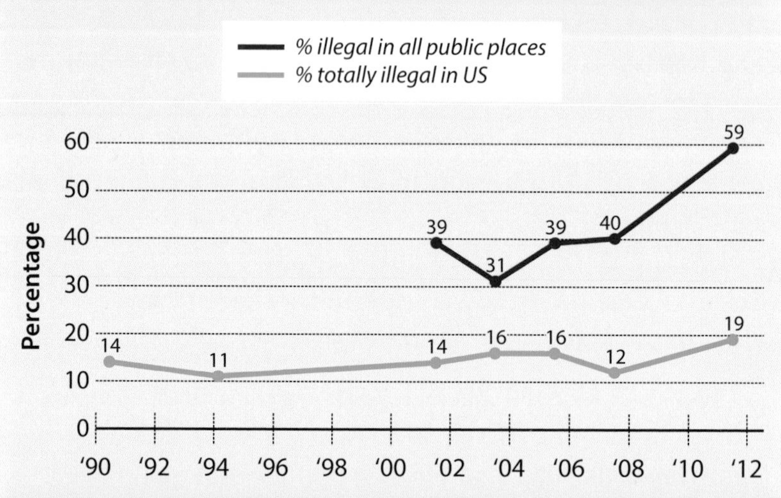

Taken from: Gallup, "For First Time, Majority in US Supports Public Smoking Ban," gallup.com, July 15, 2011.

for its ordinance, but whether its authority to enact the ban was denied by other law.

Ms. Carlson bases her argument in RSMo section 71.010. The statute limits the City's authority by providing that:

> [a]ny municipal corporation . . . having authority to pass ordinances regulating subjects, matters and things upon which there is a general law of the state . . . shall confine and restrict its jurisdiction and the passage of its ordinances to and in conformity with the state law upon the same subject.

Thus, Kansas City may only enact ordinances "in conformity" with state law on the same subject. If the city ordinance conflicts with a general law of the state, it is void.

An ordinance and state statute conflict if "their express or implied provisions are so inconsistent and irreconcilable that the statute annuls the ordinance." *Crackerneck Country Club, Inc. v. City of Independence* [1974]. . . . If the ordinance prohibits what the statute permits, or permits what the statute prohibits, then the two are in conflict. For example, where an ordinance prohibited self-service gas pumps and self-service pumping, but a state regulation expressly stated that self-service gas pumps were permitted, the ordinance was in direct conflict with the state regulation and thus invalid. However, if the ordinance merely prohibits more than the state statute, the two measures are not in conflict. In [*Kansas City v. LaRose* (1975)], a state crime required a mens rea [guilty mind] element, while a municipal ordinance did not—thus criminalizing more conduct than the state statute. However, there was no conflict between the two because the ordinance had simply "gone further" and expanded the prohibition.

Consequently, in the present case, if the ICAA were read to affirmatively permit smoking in bars and billiard parlors meeting its condition, then the municipal ordinance's prohibition would be in conflict with the state law. However, if the ordinance merely enlarges the state law, the two laws are not in conflict.

A Look at the Laws

The ICAA was enacted "to provide persons with access to smoke-free air in certain areas in certain public places." It outlaws smoking in "public places" except in designated areas. The definition of "public place" includes "any enclosed indoor area used by the general public or serving as a place of work." Several types of areas "are not considered a public place." Among the section's exclusions from the definition of "public places" are:

> Bars, taverns, restaurants that seat less than fifty people, bowling alleys and billiard parlors, which conspicuously post signs stating that 'Nonsmoking Areas are Unavailable'[.]

Thus, the ICAA does not require bars and billiard parlors such as JC's to provide non-smoking areas.

The City's municipal ban prohibits smoking in "all enclosed places of employment within the City" and in "all enclosed public places within the City." Under the ordinance, a public place is "any enclosed area to which the public is invited or in which the public is permitted." Private residences and a percentage of hotel rooms are excluded from the ordinance; casino gaming areas are exempted until surrounding counties pass similar bans. The ordinance, however, does not exempt bars and billiard parlors such as JC's from its restrictions.

Ms. Carlson argues that the ICAA's exclusion of bars and billiard parlors from its prohibition against smoking must be read as "positive law permitting that conduct, such that a city has no authority to prohibit it entirely." Thus, although the ICAA does not give express affirmative authority to JC's to permit smoking, she contends such a meaning should be implied because the ICAA exempts JC's from its definition of "public place." Consequently, she argues, the ICAA permits smoking in JC's while the ordinance prohibits it, causing the statute and the ordinance to be in conflict.

We presume ordinances are valid and lawful. We follow the principle of "ut res magis valeat quam pereat (that the thing may rather have effect than be destroyed)." We construe ordinances to be upheld "unless the ordinance is expressly inconsistent or in irreconcilable conflict with the general law of the state."

We read statutes according to their plain and ordinary language. A plain reading of the ICAA does not support Ms. Carlson's contention that it authorizes those places it exempts to permit smoking or makes them immune from local smoking regulation. Rather, the ICAA simply excludes those places meeting its conditions from compliance with section 191.767.

The failure of the legislature to include an express grant of power may establish that it intended such a power not be included. The ICAA states that its regulation of smoking in "public places" does not include bars such as JC's. It does not state, "A permit to smoke in bars is affirmatively granted." Had the

Many state and county governments have enacted Indoor Clean Air Acts that prohibit smoking in public spaces, including bars and taverns such as this one in Chevy Chase, Maryland. © Matt Houston/AP Images.

Missouri legislature intended to grant affirmative authority to these places to allow smoking, it could have so stated. Nor does the ICAA state, "Smoking in bars cannot be prohibited by cities." Had the legislature intended to prohibit municipalities from further regulation it could have so stated. Thus, we do not agree, as Ms. Carlson argues, that section 191.769(5) "specifically exempts [bars and billiard parlors] from indoor smoking regulation" such that the ordinance is in conflict.

Arguing for an Implied Authority to Permit Smoking

Ms. Carlson, however, asks us to look beyond the statute's plain language to read an implied grant of authority to permit smoking such that the city's ordinance is in conflict. She relies on several Missouri cases to argue that where a statute exempts conduct, the statute must be read as permitting that conduct, and that the ICAA's exemption of bars and billiard parlors from its ban must thus be read as an affirmative authorization of smoking in those places.

In *City of St. Louis v. Klausmeier* [1908], a municipal ordinance setting a standard requiring skimmed milk to contain 10.5 percent solids was held to conflict with a state statute that set a standard of only 9.25 percent. The conflict occurred because "a person might sell skimmed milk containing 9.25 percent of solids, as prescribed by the state law, and still be guilty of an offense under the ordinance. In other words, the ordinance denounces that to be a crime which the statute authorizes to be done." Similarly, in *City of St. Louis v. Stenson* [1960], an ordinance that prohibited commercial vehicles over thirty-three feet in length on portions of a highway was held to conflict with a statute that "authorize[d] the use of the highways . . . by all . . . vehicles that do not exceed 45 feet in length" because the ordinance prohibited what the statute permitted. However, we find neither of these cases to be directly on point. We also note that both cases were decided prior to Missouri's constitutional enactment of section 19(a).

The ICAA is a prohibitory statute: "A person shall not smoke in a public place or in a public meeting except in a designated smoking area." Section 191.769(5) excludes bars and billiard parlors from the ICAA's definition of public places, thus placing them outside section 191.767's ban. *Klausmeier* and *Stenson* do not tell us that a state exemption from a statutory prohibition is an authorization. Rather, the statutes at issue in *Klausmeier* and *Stenson* set standards for authorized conduct-the level of solids in milk, the length of motor vehicles on highways. The ordinances at issue in *Klausmeier* and *Stenson* set a different standard and expressly conflicted with the state laws because conduct was affirmatively authorized under the state law, yet illegal under the municipal ordinance.

The laws here are much more analogous to those in *LaRose* than to the standard-setting prescriptions in *Klausmeier* and *Stenson*. In *LaRose*, decided after Missouri's enactment of section

19(a), the state law prohibited conduct and the municipal ordinance prohibited more; although they prohibited the same type of conduct, because the ordinance simple went further, there was no conflict between the two.

Ms. Carlson also argues that the City is "powerless, by definition or otherwise, to embrace in the Ordinance a class of places as 'public places' for smoking regulation and subject them to penalties for violating the Ordinance, which by § 191.769(5) are within the exception of the terms of the ICAA defining the class that are in fact 'public places.'" She relies on *City of Moberly v. Hoover* [1902] . . . and *City of St. Louis v. Meyer* [1904] . . . for this argument. In *Moberly*, a bookseller was charged with failure to comply with a city ordinance levying a tax on "peddlers." Under state law, the term "peddler" was defined to exclude booksellers. The court held that the city ordinance and charter had to be construed in light of the state law and, thus, could not be read to include booksellers. Similarly, in *Meyer*, a farmer was convicted of selling his products without a license, as required by a city ordinance applying to peddlers and hawkers. However, under state law, a seller of agricultural products was not a "peddler" or a "hawker." The Meyer court found "that a class cannot be embraced in the ordinance that the statute expressly eliminates from the class defined by the statute to be peddlers."

There Is No Inherent Conflict

However, we do not agree that Missouri law holds that there is an inherent conflict where a statute and an ordinance define terms differently. Both *Meyer* and *Moberly* were decided over a century ago, in light of different constitutional provisions, and the Missouri Supreme Court has since held that state and municipal law were not inherently in conflict because of differences in their defined terms. Rather, in *Teefey* [*v. Bd. of Zoning Adjustment of Kansas City* (2000)] the Missouri Supreme Court looked to the effect of the difference in the defined terms and analyzed the issue according to the same conflict rules:

> [A] court should construe ordinances to uphold their validity unless the ordinances are expressly inconsistent or in irreconcilable conflict with the general law of the state. Ordinances may supplement state laws, but when the expressed or implied provisions of each are inconsistent or in irreconcilable conflict, then the statutes annul the ordinances. To determine if a conflict exists between an ordinance and a state statute, the test is whether the ordinance permits that which the statute prohibits or prohibits that which the statute permits.

In *Teefey*, the ordinances were not void despite the difference in defined terms because "the ordinances do not permit that which the statutes prohibit, nor do they prohibit that which the statutes permit." Because the ICAA merely excludes bars such as JC's from its proscription, it does not affirmatively permit smoking. Consequently, the ordinance does not prohibit that which the state law permits. That the two laws provide different definitions of "public place" does not by itself render the ordinance void.

VIEWPOINT 12

> *"Government-imposed smoking bans are unwise. Considered closely, the arguments used to justify them falter."*

Government-Mandated Bans on Smoking Are Not Justified

Thomas A. Lambert

In the following viewpoint, Thomas A. Lambert claims that the arguments for government-mandated bans on smoking are flawed. Indoor smoking does not violate the rights of nonsmokers because building owners may determine the amount of smoking under property rights, insists Lambert. Attempting to shape attitudes against smoking through bans, he maintains, can result in backlash and enhance tobacco's image as "rebellious" and "cool." And, Lambert alleges, the health risks of secondhand smoke touted by ban advocates are based on unsound science. He advises that a laissez-fair approach, wherein building owners accommodate the smoking preferences of their customers, would create more social welfare than sweeping bans. Lambert is Judge C.A. Leedy Professor of Law at the University of Missouri School of Law.

In recent months, dozens of localities and a number of states have enacted sweeping smoking bans. The bans generally

Thomas A. Lambert, "The Case Against Smoking Bans," *Regulation*, vol. 29, no. 4, Winter 2006, pp. 34–40.

forbid smoking in "public" places, which are defined to include not only publicly owned facilities but also privately owned properties to which members of the public are invited (e.g., bars, restaurants, hotel lobbies, etc.). Proponents of the bans insist that they are necessary to reduce risks to public health and welfare and to protect the rights of nonsmoking patrons and employees of the regulated establishments.

Specifically, ban advocates have offered three justifications for government-imposed bans: First, they claim that such bans are warranted because indoor smoking involves a "negative externality," the market failure normally invoked to justify regulation of the ambient environment. In addition, advocates assert that smoking bans shape individual preferences against smoking, thereby reducing the number of smokers in society. Finally, proponents argue that smoking bans are justified, regardless of whether any market failure is present, simply because of the health risks associated with inhalation of environmental tobacco smoke (ETS), commonly referred to as "secondhand smoke."

This [viewpoint] contends that government-imposed smoking bans cannot be justified as responses to market failure, as means of shaping preferences, or on risk-reduction grounds. Smoking bans reduce public welfare by preventing an optimal allocation of nonsmoking and smoking-permitted public places. A laissez-faire approach better accommodates heterogeneous preferences regarding public smoking.

The Externality Argument

The conventional justification for regulation of the ambient environment (i.e., outdoor air and water) is that it is necessary to combat the inefficiencies created by negative externalities. Negative externalities are costs that are not borne by the party in charge of the process that creates them. For example, the owner of a smoke-spewing factory does not fully bear the costs associated with the smoke, stench, and health risks his factory produces; many of those costs are foisted onto the factory's neighbors. When conduct involves negative externalities, participants will tend to engage in that conduct to an excessive degree, for they bear the full benefits, but not the full costs, of their activities. Quite often, then, government intervention (e.g., taxing the cost-creating behavior or limiting the amount permitted) may be desirable as a means of ensuring that the cost-creator does not engage to an excessive degree in the conduct at issue.

Advocates of smoking bans insist that indoor smoking involves negative externalities. First, ban advocates argue that nonsmoking patrons and employees of establishments that allow smoking are forced to bear costs over which they have no control. In addition, smokers impose negative externalities in the form of increased healthcare costs, a portion of which is paid from the public fisc. Thus, taxpayers are required to foot the bill for some of the costs associated with smoking in general. Examined closely, each of these externality-based arguments for smoking bans fails.

Patrons and Employees Outdoor air pollution involves the sort of negative externality likely to result in both an inoptimal (i.e., excessive) amount of the polluting activity and a violation of pollution victims' rights. When it comes to indoor air pollution, by contrast, there is no such externality. That is because the individual charged with determining how much, if any, smoking is permitted in an indoor space ultimately bears the full costs of his or her decision and is thus likely to select the optimal level of air cleanliness. Moreover, non-smokers' "rights" are not violated, because they are compensated for the inconveniences and risks they suffer.

One might wonder how this could be. Because smokers in a public space impose costs on nonsmoking patrons, who cannot order the smokers to stop, will indoor smoking not entail both the inefficiency (an excessive level of pollution) and the injustice (an infringement of non-polluters' rights to enjoy clean air) associated with outdoor air pollution? In a word, no. There

The Best Solution to Protect Public Health

It is wrong to tell businesses what legal activities they must prohibit within their own walls. The best solution to the question of how to "protect the public health" . . . is to let the public make an informed decision. A sign could be posted on the door of every business that permits smoking inside, informing the public of the presence of tobacco smoke. Restaurants already post signs at their entrances that inform prospective patrons if a microwave oven is in use. This is done to inform and warn those with pacemakers to avoid that establishment for their own safety. This is the simplest way to protect the public from secondhand smoke while not infringing on the rights of private businesses. If the business is a bar, there could be a sign that reads: "This is a smoking establishment." The message posted would be clear and just scary enough to warm the dark hearts of the fear mongers. This is by far the best solution.

Theodore J. King, The War on Smokers and the Rise of the Nanny State. *Bloomington, IN: iUniverse, 2005.*

is a crucial difference between outdoor and indoor air, and that difference alleviates the inefficiencies and rights-violations normally associated with air pollution.

The Role of Property Rights

The crucial difference is property rights. Whereas outdoor air is common property (and thus subject to the famous Tragedy of the Commons), the air inside a building is, in essence, "owned" by the building owner. That means that the building owner, who is in a position to control the amount of smoking (if any) that is permitted in the building, has an incentive to permit the "right" amount of smoking—that is, the amount that maximizes the welfare of individuals within the building. Depending on the highest and best use of the space and the types of people who patronize the building, the optimal level of smoking may be zero (as in an art museum), or "as much as patrons desire" (as in a tobacco lounge), or something in-between (as in most restaurants, which have smoking and nonsmoking sections). Because patrons select establishments based on the benefits and costs of patronage, they will avoid establishments with air policies they do not like or will, at a minimum, reduce the amount they are willing to pay for goods and services at such places. Owners of public places thus bear the full costs and benefits of their decisions regarding air quality and can be expected to select the optimal level of air cleanliness. Moreover, customers who do not like the air policy a space-owner has selected will patronize the space only if they are being otherwise compensated by some positive attribute of the space at issue—say, cheap drinks or a particularly attractive clientele. They are, in other words, compensated for any "rights" violation. The de facto property rights that exist in indoor air, then, prevent the inefficiencies and injustices that accompany outdoor air pollution.

But what about workers at businesses that permit smoking? Is there not an externality in that they are forced to bear costs (and assume risks) over which they have no control? Again, the answer is no. Workers exercise control by demanding higher pay to compensate them for the risks and unpleasantries they experience because of the smoke in their workplaces. Adam Smith theorized about such "risk premiums" when he wrote in *The Wealth of Nations:*

> The whole of the advantages and disadvantages of the different employments of labor and stock must, in the same neighborhood, be either perfectly equal or tending to equality. . . . [T]he wages of labor vary with the ease or hardship, the honorableness or dishonorableness of employment. . . .

Public Costs Ban advocates also seek to justify prohibitions by pointing to externalities in the form of public health care expenditures. The argument here proceeds as follows:

- Smokers face disproportionately high health care costs.
- A portion of such costs is borne not by smokers themselves but by the public at large.
- Smokers thereby externalize some of the costs of their behavior and thus will tend to engage in "too much" smoking.
- Therefore, smoking bans are justified as an effort to cut back on the level of smoking that would otherwise exist.

This argument suffers from several weaknesses. First and most importantly, the initial premise is unsound. According to a comprehensive study in the *New England Journal of Medicine* in 1997, smoking probably has the effect of reducing overall health care costs because smokers die earlier than nonsmokers. The study's authors concluded that in a population in which no one smoked, health care costs would be 7 percent higher among men and 4 percent higher among women than the costs in the current mixed population of smokers and nonsmokers. The authors further determined that if all smokers were to quit, health care costs would be lower at first, but after 15 years they would become higher than at present.

Even if smoking were shown to increase public health care expenditures, the argument here would seem to prove too much. If increased health care costs could justify government imposition of a smoking ban in privately owned places, could they not similarly justify governmental regulation of menus at fast food restaurants or mandatory exercise regimens? Serious liberty interests would be at stake if a government were to make its citizens "be healthy" so as not to impose health care costs on others.

Finally, the assumption that public smoking bans reduce the incidence of smoking seems suspect. As discussed below, widespread smoking bans may actually increase the incidence of smoking among young people. Externalities in the form of increased public health care costs, then, likely cannot justify widespread bans on smoking in public spaces.

Preference-Shaping Arguments Do Not Justify Public Smoking Bans

The argument above concludes that smoking bans are unnecessary because market processes will ensure either that patrons' and employees' preferences regarding smoking are honored or that those individuals are compensated for not receiving their preferences. That argument assumes, though, that individuals' preferences are unaffected by the legal rule itself. A number of scholars have disputed the notion of "exogenous preferences." Instead, they claim that individuals' preferences regarding activities like smoking are influenced by the background legal rules themselves. Some theorists have therefore sought to justify smoking bans on grounds that they make smokers less likely to want to smoke and/or make nonsmokers more likely to appreciate smoke-free environments and thus more willing to pay a premium for such environments. In the end, neither preference-shaping argument can justify widespread bans on public smoking.

Shaping Attitudes In recent years, legal scholars have produced a voluminous literature on the role of law in indirectly controlling conduct by shaping social norms and individual preferences. Smoking bans provide one of the favorite "success stories" of those who laud the use of legal rules to change norms and preferences. According to these scholars, smoking bans affect behavior, even if under-enforced, because they change the social norm regarding smoking in public. With the advent of smoking bans, nonsmokers who previously felt embarrassed about publicly expressing their distaste for ETS are speaking up. By providing a de facto community statement that public smoking is unacceptable, the bans embolden nonsmokers to confront smokers who are inconveniencing them. Facing heightened public hostility toward their habits, smokers are likely to revise their preferences regarding smoking. Thus, by making smoking more socially costly, the theory goes, bans reduce the number of smokers.

Of course, this is a good thing only if actual social utility is increased by reducing the incidence of smoking. Ban advocates assume that reducing smoking is welfare-enhancing for the obvious reason that smoking carries serious health risks. But ban advocates generally are not in a position to judge the cost side of reducing smoking because they do not know the degree of utility smokers experience by smoking. Smokers themselves, who these days are aware of the risks of smoking, appear to believe that

The Hartsfield-Jackson Atlanta International Airport has a designated smoking section. Some argue that smoking bans in public spaces are unnecessary and indoor smoking does not violate the rights of nonsmokers. © Jeff Greenberg/Alamy.

the benefits they experience from the activity outweigh the costs. It is thus not at all clear that eliminating smoking will enhance social welfare.

But even if it were clear that society would be better off with less smoking, attempting to use smoking bans to influence social norms may not represent wise policy. Sweeping smoking bans may actually increase the incidence of smoking. A large percentage of smokers acquire the habit at a young age, and they frequently do so because smoking is "cool." Smoking is cool, of course, because it is rebellious. The harder anti-smoking forces work to coerce people into quitting smoking, and the more they engage the government and other establishment institutions in their efforts, the more rebellious—and thus the "cooler"—smoking becomes. Even advocates of the use of smoking regulation to alter social norms acknowledge that overly intrusive regulations may result in this sort of "norm backlash." As an empirical matter, then, it is not clear whether sweeping smoking bans—highly intrusive regulatory interventions—actually reduce the incidence of smoking in the long run. . . .

The Risk-Based Argument Is Insufficient to Justify Smoking Bans

The first two arguments for smoking bans focus, to some degree, on citizens' preferences: the externality argument focuses on a purported market failure that allegedly prevents the satisfaction of preferences regarding smoking, and the preference-shaping argument focuses on the laws inevitable role in shaping those preferences. By contrast, the third common argument for smoking bans ignores citizens' smoking preferences altogether. That argument asserts that smoking should be banned in public places, regardless of individuals' smoking preferences, because the health risks it presents are simply too great. In other words, smoking bans are justified on risk-based grounds even if there is no need to remedy a market failure or to correct a preference-shaping bias in the law. . . .

But a purely risk-based argument likely cannot justify a sweeping smoking ban. While risk, standing alone, is sometimes deemed sufficient to justify government prohibition of private conduct, such prohibition seems appropriate only when the harm avoided is relatively great and the regulation's intrusion on personal liberty is relatively small. Again, consider mandatory seatbelt laws. The risk associated with not wearing a seatbelt is huge, and the regulation's intrusion on personal liberty is minor—no more than a slight inconvenience. Hence, the laws may be justifiable on risk-reduction grounds. Consider, by comparison, whether the government could invoke risk as a legitimate basis for banning driving after 1:00 A.M. Such behavior certainly presents a heightened risk (late-night drivers are far more likely to fall asleep at the wheel), but the magnitude of risk presented does not justify the degree of liberty intrusion occasioned by the regulation. Smoking bans look more like late-night driving bans than mandatory seatbelt laws and thus likely cannot be justified solely with reference to risk.

Isolating the Relevant Risk

To see why this is so, we must first isolate the relevant risk. Because public smoking bans do not prohibit smoking altogether and may not even reduce its incidence, the risk the bans aim to avert is not the risk to smokers themselves. It is instead the risk to nonsmokers—i.e., the risks associated with inhalation of ETS. The key question, then, is whether these risks are of sufficient magnitude to justify a significant intrusion on the personal liberty of private business owners and their customers.

If one were to rely on the stated conclusions of federal agencies (and/or the media reports discussing those conclusions), one might conclude that the risks associated with ETS inhalation do justify significant liberty restrictions. First consider the Environmental Protection Agency's 1992 report, *Respiratory Health Effects of Passive Smoking: Lung Cancer and Other Disorders*. That study, which concluded that ETS is a Class A (known human) carcinogen, purported to show that inhalation of ETS causes 3,000 lung cancer deaths per year. Not surprisingly, the study fueled efforts to impose smoking bans.

As it turns out, the study hardly amounted to sound science. A congressional inquiry into the methods the EPA used in the study found that "the process at every turn [was] characterized by both scientific and procedural irregularities," including "conflicts of interest by both Agency staff involved in the preparation of the risk assessment and members of the Science Advisory Board panel selected to provide a supposedly independent evaluation of the document." The congressional inquiry further concluded that "the Agency ha[d] deliberately abused and manipulated the scientific data in order to reach a predetermined, politically motivated result."...

Apparently undeterred by these congressional and judicial reprimands, the U.S. surgeon general recently released a report entitled *The Health Consequences of Involuntary Exposure to Tobacco Smoke*, which purports to settle once and for all the debate over the risks of ETS inhalation. In releasing the report, Surgeon General Richard Carmona confidently proclaimed:

> The scientific evidence is now indisputable: secondhand smoke is not a mere annoyance. It is a serious health hazard that can lead to disease and premature death in children and nonsmoking adults.

In presenting the report, the surgeon general's office emphasized to the news media that even brief exposure to ETS poses immediate and significant health risks. The press release accompanying the report stated that "there is no risk-free level of exposure to secondhand smoke" and that "even brief exposure to secondhand smoke has immediate adverse effects on the cardiovascular system and increases risk for heart disease and lung cancer." In his remarks to the media, the surgeon general stated, "Breathing secondhand smoke for even a short time can damage cells and set the cancer process in motion." In a "fact sheet" accompanying the report, the surgeon general explained, "Breathing secondhand smoke for even a short time can have immediate adverse effects on the cardiovascular system." These and similar statements, faithfully repeated by the news media, create the impression that science has determined that simply being in a smoke-filled room exposes one to significant health risks.

Examined closely, the surgeon general's report established no such proposition. The underlying studies upon which the surgeon general's report was based considered the effects of chronic exposure to ETS on individuals, such as long-time spouses of smokers. The studies simply did not consider the health effects of sporadic exposure to ETS and thus cannot provide empirical support for the surgeon general's statements about short-term ETS exposure. . . .

But what about the actual findings of the surgeon general's report, as opposed to the hyperbolic (and widely reported) accompanying statements? Those findings—even taken at face value—do not provide a risk-based rationale for highly intrusive smoking bans. The report concludes that chronic ETS exposure increases the risks of lung cancer and heart disease by 20 to 30 percent. While those numbers sound fairly large, one must remember that the underlying risks of lung cancer and heart disease in nonsmokers are quite small to begin with. A 20 percent increase in a tiny risk is, well, really tiny—certainly too tiny to justify the substantial liberty infringement involved in smoking bans. Indeed, risk alone has not justified a ban on smoking itself, an activity that increases the risk of heart disease by 100 to 300 percent and that of lung cancer by 900 percent. How, then, could a much smaller risk justify highly intrusive regulation of the voluntary actions of individuals gathered on private property? . . .

The Superiority of the Laissez-Faire Approach

Controversies over smoking in public places are ultimately controversies over property rights. Does a smoker have the right to fill the air with his or her smoke, or do nonsmokers have the right to smoke-free air? In other words, who "owns" the air? A smoking ban effectively gives nonsmoking patrons the right to the air. By contrast, the laissez-faire approach effectively permits the owner of the establishment to determine the proper allocation of air rights within his or her space. The owner may choose to give the rights to smoking patrons (by permitting smoking), nonsmokers (by banning smoking), or to try to accommodate both by designating some parts of the establishment nonsmoking but permitting smoking elsewhere within the space.

However owners allocate the right to air among smokers and nonsmokers, there will be some "winners" whose preferred policy is adopted and whose happiness is therefore increased, and some "losers" whose preferred policy is rejected and whose happiness is therefore diminished. There is thus, as [economist] Ronald Coase explained, an unavoidable reciprocal harm inherent in any allocation of the right to the indoor air at issue. Adoption of a smoking-permitted policy harms nonsmokers, but adoption of a no-smoking policy harms smokers.

In light of this unavoidable, reciprocal harm, social welfare would be maximized if smoking policies were set to favor the group whose total happiness would be most enhanced by implementation of its favored policy. So, if smoking customers value the right to smoke in a particular place more than nonsmoking customers value the right to be free from such smoke, that place should allow smoking. Conversely, if nonsmoking patrons value an establishment's clean air more than smoking patrons value the right to light up, the establishment should ban smoking.

It should thus be clear why a laissez-faire approach of permitting establishment owners to set their own smoking policies will create more welfare than a ban on smoking in public places. Under the laissez-faire approach, a business owner, seeking to maximize his or her profits, will set the establishment's smoking policy to accommodate the patrons who most value their preferred policy (and thus are most willing to pay a premium to be in the proprietor's space). This will result in a variety of smoking policies at different establishments, as business owners respond to the preferences of their customers.

Under a smoking ban, by contrast, business owners are not permitted to cater to smoking patrons' demands even when those patrons value the right to smoke more than nonsmoking patrons (and employees) value the right to be free from smoke. A smoking ban, then, is less likely to maximize social welfare than a laissez-faire approach, which ensures that the right to any particular public place's air is allocated to the group that values it most.

Government-imposed smoking bans are unwise. Considered closely, the arguments used to justify them falter. The externality argument fails because indoor smoking creates, at worst, a pecuniary externality that will be mitigated by the price mechanism. Preference-shaping arguments are weak because heavy-handed government restrictions create a substantial risk of "norm backlash." Risk-based arguments are insufficient because the slight risks associated with ETS cannot justify the substantial privacy intrusion occasioned by sweeping smoking bans. In the end, a laissez-faire policy that would permit private business owners to tailor their own smoking policies according to the demands of their patrons is most likely to maximize social welfare by providing an optimal allocation of both smoking and smoke-free establishments.

"We forget that habits such as smoking can irreversibly affect those around us, whether they are our friends, family members, children or complete strangers."

Banning Smoking on College Campuses Benefits Student Health

Stacey Oparnica

In the following viewpoint, Stacy Oparnica writes that prohibiting smoking at colleges and universities would promote student health and prevent young people from starting the habit. The author contends that tobacco is the leading cause of premature and preventable deaths in the United States, and exposure to secondhand smoke increases the risk of heart disease. Student opposition to the policy is equally objectionable to smoking due to its irreversible consequences on others, she argues. At the time of publication, Oparnica was a journalism major at San Diego State University in California.

Cigarettes—chances are you either smoke them or despise them. Whatever your stance on "cancer sticks" may be, it's safe to say it's becoming increasingly difficult for people to

Stacey Opernica, "UC Smoking Ban Is Step Forward for Health," *Daily Aztec*, January 23, 2012.

light up in public. It began in 1995 when California became the first state to execute a smoking ban in most indoor work sites in an effort to prevent employees from being subjected to secondhand smoke.

Roughly two decades later, similar legislation is being introduced by the University of California system and it's guaranteed to garner both tremendous support and backlash.

The proposed ordinance calls for a total ban on smoking and all tobacco-related products for students and faculty alike on all 10 UC campuses, which will be implemented within the next two years, according to UC President Mark Yudof. Administrators from each of the 10 universities will make their own decisions regarding certain policy specifications, but the general goal is for each UC campus to be a smoke-free environment by 2014.

Although this decision may seem rather drastic to some, at least one student is breathing a sigh of relief. "I'm a nonsmoker and I hate having to walk around campus and hold my breath as I go by (someone who's smoking)," Haylee Clay, a communications junior at San Diego State, said. "If someone wants to kill their lungs, that's their problem, not mine. But I don't want it anywhere near me. I'm all for the ban."

It should come as no surprise that a significant number of people share Clay's frustration with cigarettes. In fact, 59 percent of Americans supported a smoking ban in all public places in a Gallup Poll last year [in 2011], increased from 39 percent in 2001. Still, those opposed to the ban are spewing fiery criticism concerning students and faculty being robbed of their right to smoke: It's their choice, after all, and a legal choice at that. However, nonsmokers have rights, too, do they not?

Smoking Irreversibly Affects Society

We are all well aware cigarettes contain carcinogens, or cancer-causing agents. But did you know tobacco-related use accounts for more deaths than those from HIV, illegal drug use, car accidents, suicides and murders combined? Every year in the United

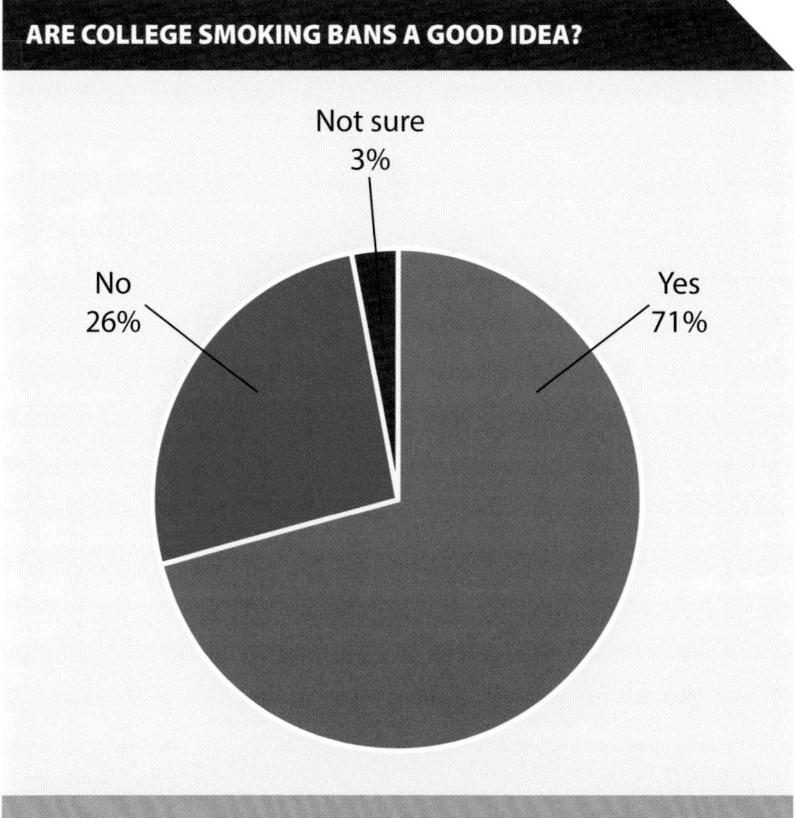

Taken from: "UC Smoking Ban Is Step Forward for Health," *Daily Aztec*. www.thedailyaztec.com.

States, 443,000 people die from smoking, which is still the number one cause of preventable, premature deaths in our country. Let those words simmer in your mind for a moment: preventable and premature.

More than likely, you've heard this information before. But how much do you actually know about secondhand smoke? After all, if you're a smoker yourself, shouldn't you be actively aware of how the cigarette resting between your fingers is affecting the health of those around you? Well, I'll tell you exactly how. Nearly 46,000 Americans die each year because of heart disease from secondhand smoke, according to the American Cancer Society.

Students gather on the University of Kentucky campus to protest the school's smoking ban in 2009. Many believe that banning smoking on school campuses promotes health and reduces the number of young people who will develop an addiction to smoking. © David Perry/The Lexington Herald-Leader/AP Images.

"Even brief exposure can be dangerous because nonsmokers inhale many of the same poisons in cigarette smoke as smokers," the Centers for Disease Control stated.

I'll be honest and tell you I've smoked a significant number of cigarettes in my life, much to the disgust and dismay of my older sister who never once let a cigarette touch her lips. The most shameful part, though? If you were to ask me whether or not I've smoked around someone with asthma or around a child, I wouldn't even know what to say because, truthfully, I hardly paid attention to those around me before lighting up. That's what happens when a terrible habit becomes a customary and acceptable part of our culture—we forget how terrible it actually is. We forget that habits such as smoking can irreversibly affect those around us, whether they are our friends, family members, children or complete strangers. How do we justify that? We can't.

It might infuriate you Yudof has decided you can no longer enjoy your mentholated Kools during breaks between classes. It might make your fingers tremble and your blood boil. However, if eliminating secondhand smoke on campus and perhaps even discouraging incoming freshmen from picking up the habit are possible outcomes of this decision, then opposing the ban for the sake of your mid-break cigarette is even more disgusting than the habit itself.

Viewpoint 14

"The reasoning behind the policy is to keep smoking out in the open, and not have teachers tracking down smokers in school bathrooms and hallways."

A High School Designated Smoking Area Causes Controversy

John Hilliard

In the following viewpoint, John Hilliard states that a recent policy designating a smoking area off campus at a Massachusetts high school has divided local officials. School administrators, Hilliard maintains, contend that monitoring the habit on campus diverts human resources, and the policy keeps smoking visible, refers smokers to cessation programs, and protects students from secondhand smoke. However, numerous health officials oppose it, arguing that the policy sends a mixed message to teens about smoking, counters effective antismoking efforts, and enables the tobacco industry to target youths. As for the students, Hilliard explains that most support having a smoking area near campus, but some doubt that it

John Hillard, "Despite Health Risks, New Policy Tolerates Student Smoking Outside Brookline High," *Wicked Local Brookline*, September 20, 2010.

encourages smoking students to quit. The author is a staff writer for the Wicked Local Brookline, *a community news website in Norfolk County, Massachusetts.*

Smoking may be anathema to school health education, but students can light up close to the Brookline High School campus this year under a new policy that grants smokers a spot across from the school's front doors and gymnasium.

The reasoning behind the policy is to keep smoking out in the open, and not have teachers tracking down smokers in school bathrooms and hallways, said the high school's headmaster, Bob Weintraub.

"The schools banning smoking entirely have to allocate significant human resources to inside or outside the school, wherever smoking takes place," said Weintraub, later noting that some schools have teachers monitoring bathrooms for smokers.

"To me, I'd rather have the teachers at Brookline High School working on more productive activities," said Weintraub.

But critics of the policy said it's contrary to years of teaching students about the risks of smoking.

"It's a very mixed message [to students]. We'd hope that school systems would spend all their efforts highlighting the dangers of smoking, and not tolerate any opportunity to smoke," said Marc Hymovitz, director of government outreach for the American Cancer Society in Boston, who noted that no one under age 18 can legally buy cigarettes in Massachusetts.

Under the new policy, the school encourages students who smoke to do so on the sidewalk at the corner of Greenough Street and Davis Avenue.

In the school's handbook, the spot is officially "off campus," but the sidewalk is flanked on one side by the school's ballfield, and faces the main entrances to the gym and high school building. Greenough Street is also closed to vehicle traffic during the day to make it easier for students to come and go between classes.

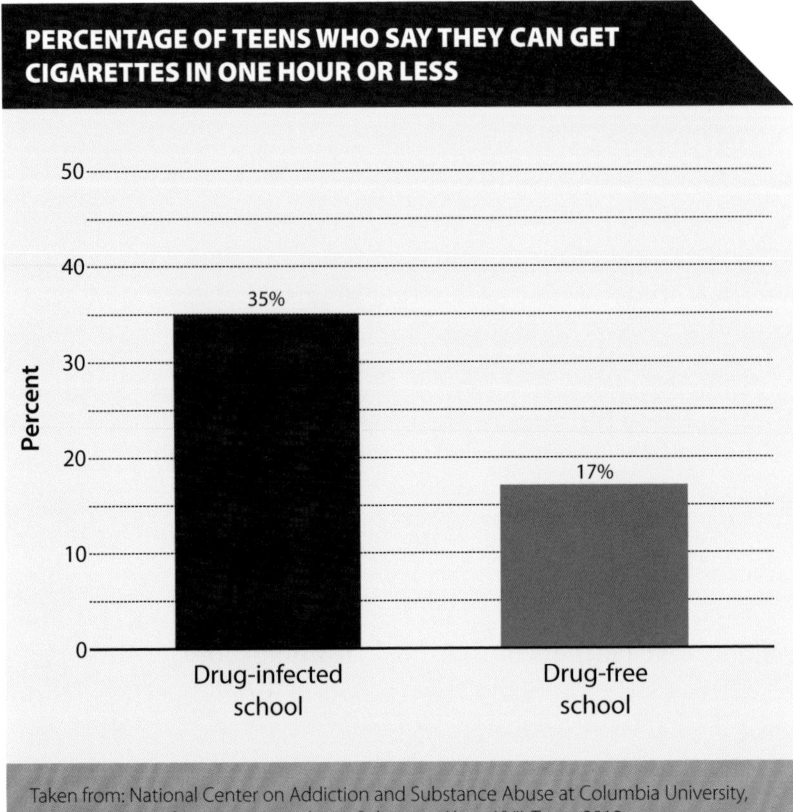

Taken from: National Center on Addiction and Substance Abuse at Columbia University, *National Survey of American Attitudes on Substance Abuse XVII: Teens*, 2012. www.casacolumbia.org.

Mary Minott, the high school's coordinator of substance abuse prevention, said three school staffers go out to any student smokers and let them know about the assistance programs that are available. She said that anecdotally, there appear to be fewer smokers at the school than in the past since the policy began with the new school year.

"It's a health problem. We don't try to turn it into [an issue of] 'You're a bad person because you have an addiction,'" said Minott.

The school can't stop students who smoke on the public sidewalk at the corner of Tappan and Greenough streets, but officials ask students to move out of the way, she said.

Minott said this policy doesn't apply to adults smoking on the sidewalk.

While the school can't prevent freshmen from smoking on public property, the school changed its "open campus" policy to prevent first-semester freshmen from leaving school grounds. Older students, and second-semester freshmen with parental consent, can leave school grounds during the day.

The school's policy bans smoking on official school property, including the Cypress Street playing field. The sidewalk along the field is not school-controlled property.

"Kids Spot Hypocrisy a Mile Away"

The school developed the policy with the input of about 30 juniors and seniors, along with substance abuse prevention staff, in response to a forum hosted last year with Brookline Coalition Against Substance Abuse.

But that policy raised the ire of some anti-smoking advocates, who said the measure is contrary to what's proven to reduce smoking rates among teens.

Danny McGoldrick, vice president of research for the Washington, D.C.-based Campaign for Tobacco-Free Kids, said the Brookline policy contradicts anti-smoking efforts.

"Kids spot hypocrisy a mile away," said McGoldrick, who later added, "If you carve out an area that is OK to smoke, you're contradicting your message in other venues."

He said the Centers for Disease Control and Prevention and other health agencies encourage a single message on the risks of smoking that is directed to young people.

"It's not a normal behavior. It kills half of those who do it in their lifetime," said McGoldrick of smoking.

Hymovitz, of the American Cancer Society in Boston, criticized the policy for "making it easier and more tolerable" to smoke.

"It's counter to all of the proven tobacco control efforts over the past several years, and it plays into the hands of the

Some high school policies allow smoking in designated areas on school grounds so that students will feel less compelled to leave campus or sneak around in order to smoke. © Simone Becchetti/Getty Images.

tobacco industry" because they are looking for young smokers, said Hymovitz.

He said the state's 2004 ban on workplace smoking was successful by making it harder for people to smoke, and gave them an incentive to quit. He said educational efforts to highlight the dangers of smoking, smoking bans in schools and higher taxes on cigarettes have had a similar effect on youth smoking figures.

"It seems like a backwards policy to make it easier for children to smoke," said Hymovitz.

According to a study of tobacco use among young people conducted by the state departments of public health and K–12 education, which reviewed data from 1993 through 2009, about 82 percent of adult smokers in Massachusetts began smoking before age 19.

Statewide, about 17 percent of high schoolers in 2009 had used a tobacco product within the previous 30 days of taking a tobacco use survey, according to the report.

However, the report showed tobacco use statewide was higher among older high schoolers: in 2009, about 11 percent of freshmen smoke, and by senior year, that figure increased to 21 percent.

Cigarette smoking causes about 8,000 deaths each year in Massachusetts, according to the report. Officials also worry that smoking at a young age increases the chances of picking up riskier addictions such as drugs later in life.

"Our Job Is to Embrace a Whole Range of Kids"

In Brookline, about 9 percent of high schoolers—roughly 170 students—smoked within 30 days of the most recent youth risk survey the school conducted, according to Weintraub.

"I have an attitude you don't want to push kids away from the school . . . our job is to embrace a whole range of kids," said Weintraub.

Alan Balsam, the town's health director, acknowledged that the school's new smoking policy isn't a "perfect message," but regards it as a step forward in grappling with student smoking and protecting others from the dangers of smoking.

The school used to ban smoking, and students would gather on nearby public property, he said. The new policy was meant to eliminate that "gauntlet" of smokers that nonsmokers had to pass through every day to get to school.

"Part of this is recognizing that there are kids who smoke, and we want to protect the kids who don't smoke" from secondhand smoking risks, said Balsam.

"We're monitoring the tobacco use among youngsters, and I'm feeling pretty good" about those rates when compared to other communities, said Balsam.

The *TAB* [newspaper] attempted to speak to a representative with the state Department of Public Health's Tobacco Control Program, but a spokeswoman would only accept written questions in advance from the *TAB* via e-mail. She declined to make a representative available over the phone.

While Brookline allows students to smoke across the street from the school, other school districts continue to frown on any tobacco use near a school.

In Newton, a city ordinance prohibits smoking within 300 yards of the Newton North High School building, with penalties for repeat offenses, including fines of up to $200 and smoking cessation classes.

Waltham High School's citywide ban on tobacco products on school property includes harsher punishments. For a first offense, a student will be slapped with an overnight suspension from school, a meeting with the principal before returning to classes and attendance at two tobacco education classes.

Watertown High School students caught smoking on school grounds face suspension, while Wellesley High School bans all tobacco products from school property.

"We're Not Doing Drugs"

At Brookline High School, during a warm early afternoon last week, dozens of students lingered around the athletic field in front of the school, though none appeared to be smoking. Students who spoke with the *TAB* were mixed on the new policy, but generally agreed with allowing students the option to smoke on campus.

"It makes sense—it stops the freshmen from smoking," said Jesse Schneider, a junior who said he smokes.

He thought the policy was inconvenient; it forces students under shade trees in nice weather, and smokers can't spread out at all. He was skeptical about whether it would encourage smokers to quit.

"It's really not having an effect on me," Schneider said.

Senior Myles Grimes, who said he smokes, agreed with the policy and said school officials are taking the new policy seriously.

"They're taking it offensively if we do smoke" in other areas, he said.

"It's understandable, but it's something that shouldn't be limited—we're not doing drugs," said Tyrone Nunez, a junior who smokes. He later noted that cutting down on smoking at the school doesn't mean students have kicked the habit.

"It does help [students] to smoke less, but it doesn't stop smoking," he said.

Two other seniors, Marni Musmon and Alex Sanchez, said the policy was better than an outright smoking ban. Neither smoke, they said.

"I think it's fair. A lot of schools don't allow smoking at all," said Musmon.

"And if you did, kids would find a way" to smoke, said Sanchez.

"I hate it, it sucks . . . people don't really like it," said Gabriel Toledo, a junior at Brookline High School.

Toledo, a smoker who said the school's previous smoking policy was better because it gave smokers more freedom of movement, said the policy was made to keep students away from where younger kids and parents had to walk.

While the measure has limited where smokers can light up, the school hasn't stopped student smoking, either.

"They're letting us smoke here," said Toledo. "It's a plus."

One high school student agreed to be interviewed, and told a reporter he was a smoker. When asked for his name, he declined, and said he said his mother might learn that he smokes if he gave his name to the paper.

VIEWPOINT 15

> *"Lighting up a few cigarettes can ultimately turn your life upside-down."*

A Teen Discusses How Smoking Caused Her Brother Harm

E.S.

In the following viewpoint, E.S. narrates how her brother's choice to smoke resulted in drug use and other negative impacts on his life. Her brother went from smoking a few cigarettes a week to a pack a day and then became addicted to marijuana, leading to problems in school, personality changes, and rehab, she says. He no longer uses marijuana and can legally smoke cigarettes now, E.S. claims, but he lost his motivation to achieve. In retrospect, she maintains that smoking only worsens one's problems and can be a source of anger, guilt, and sadness. At the time of publication, the author was a teen living in Edina, Minnesota.

My brother started smoking when he was in seventh grade. He only had a few cigarettes a week, about a pack a month. Then his usage increased. It didn't seem drastic; he probably had one more cigarette each week, until it turned into a pack a week, then a pack a day. He claimed he wasn't addicted and could quit whenever he wanted. It was just something to do with his friends that relaxed him, or so he thought. My dad tried to help him quit, but how could he when my dad works nine or ten hours a day and school gets out at two? Alex thought he could trick everyone by taking a shower, using mouthwash or spraying on tons of cologne after he smoked. But his clothes reeked of fumes, and finally he didn't try to hide it. I was concerned for him, but I was a bit oblivious—until he got in too deep.

The instant I met Alex's friend Joe, I didn't like him. He seemed greasy and sneaky, not someone I wanted to associate with. Well, my brother did—for one reason. Joe had pot he was willing to share with my brother. They taught me how to measure and roll it while I watched in disgust. We'd go on walks at night and they'd smoke the joints they had slowly perfected. I knew it was wrong and illegal, but I never told anyone. One reason I didn't tell was because I never got along with my brother, but when he was high he treated me like a friend, not a lowly little sister. Plus, I felt a special bond because we had a secret. Once when I was going to tell my dad, Alex's best friend said, "If you tell your dad, Alex won't like you anymore." I had the biggest crush on this guy, so I believed him. I certainly didn't want my brother to hate me.

Smoking Makes Problems Worse

After a couple of weeks of using pot, his actions changed. He missed school, claiming he was sick, but I knew he was just tired. Every night he snuck out with friends and smoked. Soon he started acting like a jerk to everyone, including me, so I didn't like him smoking anymore. He was really depressed before he started smoking and the pot just made it worse. Eventually he had to go to a rehab center to help him quit. It worked for a while, but then he started again. It's been a hard struggle.

I'm proud to say my brother no longer does pot, but he does still smoke cigarettes. Now that he's 18, I guess he isn't breaking

A Principal Gateway Drug

It is now understood that early use of tobacco is one of the best indications that adolescents are now using or will use alcohol and the illegal drugs in the future. Young people who smoke in middle school and high school are much more likely to also use other drugs, and young people who don't smoke are much less likely to use any other drugs. Tobacco's addictive properties, the health consequences associated with tobacco use, the burdensome costs of unnecessary medical expenses and productivity losses, and tobacco's role as a principal gateway drug all provide compelling reasons for intensive prevention efforts targeting tobacco.

Richard Wilson and Cheryl Kolander, Drug Abuse Prevention: A School and Community Partnership, *third edition. Sudbury, MA: Jones and Bartlett Publishers, 2011.*

the law. I still worry because he has no motivation in life, thanks to the drugs. He's really smart and I know he could be successful if he put his mind to it. This just shows that lighting up a few cigarettes can ultimately turn your life upside-down.

The things my brother has gone through taught me several things. First, you should always tell an adult if you know someone who is doing drugs. I carry the guilt that I could have helped my brother earlier if I had said something. I also learned that smoking does not solve problems; it just makes them worse. In fact, it adds problems. And lastly, I learned I never want to touch a cigarette, or a joint, because I have seen the anger, guilt and sadness it can cause. Smoking is a major health issue among teens. Something has to be done. If not, what will become of all the promising young people in the world?

VIEWPOINT

"Even without adding tobacco to its list of regulatory efforts, the FDA is struggling to carry out its other responsibilities, including the safety of the nation's food, drugs and medical devices."

Authorizing the Food and Drug Administration to Regulate the Tobacco Industry Is Problematic

Craig A. Conway

In 2009 President Barack Obama signed the Family Smoking Prevention and Tobacco Control Act into law. In the following viewpoint, Craig A. Conway claims that the act reverses the US Supreme Court's decision nine years earlier to prohibit the Food and Drug Administration (FDA) from regulating tobacco. According to the author, the FDA is already struggling to keep pace with the increasing demands to ensure the safety of food and pharmaceuticals. The new restrictions on tobacco products under the act—from label requirements to restrictions on marketing that target youth—divert the FDA's strained resources from these responsibilities, he insists. Furthermore, the author states, the act's prohibitions on advertising may infringe on tobacco companies' free speech rights.

Craig A. Conway, "FDA Gains Regulatory Authority over Tobacco," *Health Law Perspectives*, July 2009.

Conway is a research professor at the University of Houston Law Center's Health Law and Policy Institute.

On June 22, 2009, President [Barack] Obama signed into law the Family Smoking Prevention and Tobacco Control Act (the Act), giving the U.S. Food and Drug Administration (FDA) the power to regulate the tobacco industry. Passed by sizable majorities in both the House and the Senate and supported by the American Cancer Society, healthcare professionals, and even some tobacco manufacturers, the Act reverses the 2000 United States Supreme Court's decision in *FDA v. Brown & Williamson Tobacco Corp.*, which held the government agency lacked authority to regulate tobacco products. For decades, the agency's attempt to take on Big Tobacco has been thwarted through adverse legal decisions, lobbying efforts and unsuccessful legislative action. Now that the FDA has been given the regulatory power, some question the agency's ability to effectively govern at a time when its resources and manpower are being stretched beyond capacity.

© John Deering/Cartoonist Group.

A Background on Tobacco

According to the Centers for Disease Control and Prevention, approximately 443,000 deaths are attributable to cigarette smoking each year and nearly 1,000 children become new, regular smokers every day. Moreover, tobacco manufacturers spend about $40 million every day to market its products, particularly to children, by promoting "enticing candy and fruit-flavored cigarettes," according to a study by the American Cancer Society Cancer Action Network. It is widely known the lobbying power of tobacco manufacturers is highly effective, and thus, legislative efforts to regulate tobacco products have failed to yield much success.

In the late 1950s, only 44 percent of Americans believed smoking caused cancer. That number jumped to 78 percent by 1968. A 1964 Surgeon General report on smoking and health had a major impact on public attitudes and policy over the course of that decade. Yet, while the 1964 report concluded that "cigarette smoking is a health hazard of sufficient importance in the United States to warrant appropriate remedial action," it failed to provide specific recommendations. That challenge fell to politicians. While a battle among legislators and tobacco manufacturers has raged since, substantive regulations and legislation intending to control the tobacco industry have failed to pass. Instead, incremental measures have been passed. For example, in 1965, Congress required all cigarette packages distributed in the United States to carry a health warning, and since 1970, this warning has been made in the name of the Surgeon General. In 1970, cigarette advertising on television and radio was banned.

In the past 15 years, the FDA has taken steps to aggressively assert its influence in the tobacco industry. Tasked with "protecting the public health by assuring the safety, efficacy and security of human and veterinary drugs, biological products, medical devices, our nation's food supply, cosmetics and products that emit radiation," the FDA launched a sizeable effort in 1996 to

US president Barack Obama signs the Family Smoking Prevention and Tobacco Control Act into law on June 22, 2009. The bill authorizes the Food and Drug Administration to regulate the tobacco industry. © Mark Wilson/Getty Images.

significantly regulate cigarettes and tobacco products, and control the marketing of those products to children and adolescents. The agency's regulatory measure was successfully challenged legally by Big Tobacco.

Reversing a Supreme Court Decision

In 1996, former head of the FDA, David Kessler, launched a daring initiative to assert regulatory authority over tobacco after decades of deliberately avoiding the task. Kessler, and the FDA, reasoned that nicotine was a "drug" within the meaning of the Food, Drug, and Cosmetic Act, and that cigarettes and smokeless tobacco are "devices," i.e., "combination products" (which the agency had statutory authority to regulate) designed to deliver the drug, nicotine, to the body. In response, the agency promulgated regulations intending to reduce tobacco consumption among children and teenagers, widely believed by the FDA to be a target group of the tobacco companies.

A group of tobacco manufacturers, retailers, and advertisers filed suit in federal court challenging the regulations as exceeding the FDA's authority. A threshold issue for the United State Supreme Court was determining the appropriate framework for analyzing the FDA's assertion of regulatory authority over tobacco.

Writing for the Court, Justice Sandra Day O'Connor said the "case involves one of the most troubling public health problems facing our Nation today: the thousands of premature deaths that occur each year because of tobacco use." Although a majority of the Court in the 5 to 4 decision expressed concern over the economic and health costs attributed to tobacco use, it refused to grant the FDA regulatory authority "in a manner that is inconsistent with the administrative structure that Congress enacted into law."

In a comprehensive and meticulously-written opinion, Justice O'Connor thoroughly examined FDA's proposed regulations, the statutory authority granted to the agency by Congress, as well as other federal laws and Congressional intent. For example, Justice O'Connor wrote "it is clear that Congress intended to exclude tobacco products from the FDA's jurisdiction." She reasoned:

> [A] fundamental precept of the FDCA [the Food, Drug, and Cosmetic Act] is that any product regulated by the FDA that remains on the market must be safe and effective for its intended use. . . That is, the potential for inflicting death or physical injury must be offset by the possibility of therapeutic

> benefit. . . . In its rulemaking proceeding, the FDA quite exhaustively documented that tobacco products are unsafe, dangerous, and cause great pain and suffering from illness. These findings logically imply that, if tobacco products were "devices" under the FDCA, the FDA would be required to remove them from the market. . . . Congress, however, has foreclosed a ban of such products, choosing instead to create a distinct regulatory scheme focusing on the labeling and advertising of cigarettes and smokeless tobacco. Its express policy is to protect commerce and the national economy while informing consumers about any adverse health effects. Thus, an FDA ban would plainly contradict congressional intent. . . .

The Court concluded by reiterating the serious health concerns raised by tobacco use and the FDA's attempt to address the problem. "The agency has amply demonstrated that tobacco use, particularly among children and adolescents, poses perhaps the single most significant threat to public health in the United States," wrote Justice O'Connor. Nonetheless, Justice O'Connor wrote, an "administrative agency's power to regulate in the public interest must always be grounded in a valid grant of authority from Congress." The Court failed to find such power delegated to the FDA by Congress. Nine years later, the recently-enacted Family Smoking Prevention and Tobacco Control Act reverses the Court's decision and remedies the lack of regulatory authority conferred on the agency.

A Look at the Act's Provisions

One major provision of the Act establishes the Center for Tobacco Products, a unit within the FDA dedicated to carrying out the law's provisions. Funded by user fees from tobacco manufacturers and importers, the Center will have the authority to require that all ingredients, compounds, and additives in tobacco products be reported to the agency, and ban products found to be harmful. Although menthol, nicotine, and cigarettes as a whole cannot be banned outright, cigarettes with fruit, mint, or other flavoring are. Additionally, new tobacco products failing to meet FDA pre-market standards will not enter the market. The new law also gives the FDA authority to do the following:

- require disclosure of a tobacco product's contents;
- compel the tobacco industry to research the effect of its products on consumers' health;
- prohibit terms such as "light," "mild," and "low-tar" on tobacco products;
- require warning labels to cover 50 percent of the front and rear of each pack, with the word "warning" in capital letters.

A significant aspect of the law seeks to reduce targeting of tobacco products through marketing, advertising, and other promotional efforts to children and adolescents. Tobacco companies are thus no longer allowed to sponsor sporting events and outdoor advertising of tobacco products is no longer allowed within 1,000 feet of a school. Whether such advertising restrictions placed on a company can survive a First Amendment legal challenge remains to be seen. Although Representative Henry Waxman said the legislation was carefully drafted to avoid such litigation, many first amendment advocacy groups expect there to be legal challenges to the Act's advertising restrictions.

In the meantime, FDA Commissioner, Margaret Hamburg, has stated she is eager to undertake her new role. "We now have an opportunity to really make a difference with what is probably the No. 1 public health concern in the nation and the world," said Hamburg. However, some commentators note that the FDA is badly underfunded, understaffed, and needs to act more aggressively when threats to the public's health arise.

Can the FDA Handle Big Tobacco?

In recent months, Congress has increased the budget of the FDA to coincide with the agency's new role in regulating tobacco, and President Obama is asking for additional funding. However, a recent Government Accountability Office (GAO) report notes that the agency's resources have not kept pace with "the growing demands placed on it."

The report noted that the FDA may only inspect about eight percent of nearly 3,300 estimated foreign drug-manufacturers subject to inspection in a given year. "As a result, the American consumer may not be adequately protected from unsafe and ineffective medical products," the report concluded.

Recent health issues attributed to cookie dough, pistachios, and imported peppers—all of which the FDA is tasked to monitor—have added to the mounting concerns regarding the agency's ability to effectively do its job.

Even without adding tobacco to its list of regulatory efforts, the FDA is struggling to carry out its other responsibilities, including the safety of the nation's food, drugs and medical devices. The new Center for Tobacco Products will undoubtedly divert resources from other centers and may even further sidetrack oversight efforts of clinical trials and the post-market safety monitoring of medical products.

Seemingly aware of its strained resources, the FDA recently asked "all interested parties to provide information and share views" on its implementation of the new Act. Specifically, the agency said it is interested in "comments on the approaches and actions the agency should consider initially to increase the likelihood of reducing the incidence and prevalence of tobacco use and protecting the public health." Hopefully, the agency will be up to the task.

Organizations to Contact

The editors have compiled the following list of organizations concerned with the issues debated in this book. The descriptions are derived from materials provided by the organizations. All have publications or information available for interested readers. The list was compiled on the date of publication of the present volume; the information provided here may change. Be aware that many organizations take several weeks or longer to respond to inquiries, so allow as much time as possible.

Action on Smoking and Health (ASH)
701 4th Street NW
Washington, DC 20001
(202) 659-4310 • fax: (202) 289-7166
e-mail: info@ash.org
website: http://ash.org

Established in 1967, ASH has a long history of advocacy, education, and legal initiatives in the fight against tobacco. It has fought for health in courts, before legislative bodies, and regulatory agencies as well as international agencies such as the United Nations and the World Health Organization. ASH publishes policy papers, such as "Tobacco: Not an Ordinary Product," and fact sheets.

American Legacy Foundation
1724 Massachusetts Avenue NW
Washington, DC 20036
(202) 454-5555
e-mail: info@americanlegacy.org
website: www.legacyforhealth.org

The American Legacy Foundation is dedicated to building a world where young people reject tobacco, and anyone can quit using tobacco. The foundation works on the antitobacco truth campaign, which focuses on youth prevention and education.

It conducts extensive research on tobacco-related issues and publishes the results in its *First Look Reports*, a series of brief summaries of its research.

American Lung Association

1301 Pennsylvania Avenue NW, Suite 800
Washington, DC 20004
(202) 785-3355 • fax: (202) 452-1805
website: www.lung.org

Founded in 1904 as the National Association for the Study and Prevention of Tuberculosis, the American Lung Association was among the first to tackle smoking as a preventable health risk. Landmark victories included The Clean Air Act, which banned smoking on airplanes and gave the US Food and Drug Administration authority over the marketing, sale, and manufacturing of tobacco products. Its publications include *Too Many Cases, Too Many Deaths: Lung Cancer in African Americans and State of Tobacco Control Report 2011–12*, which are available online.

Americans for Nonsmokers' Rights (ANR)

2530 San Pablo Avenue, Suite J
Berkeley, CA 94702
(510) 841-3032 • fax: (510) 841-3071
website: www.no-smoke.org

ANR is a national lobbying organization dedicated to nonsmokers' rights, taking on the tobacco industry at all levels of government, protecting nonsmokers from exposure to secondhand smoke, and preventing tobacco addiction among youth. ANR pursues an action-oriented program of policy and legislation. It publishes a quarterly newsletter, *UPDATE!*, and provides information on a variety of smoke-free issues.

Campaign for Tobacco-Free Kids

1400 I Street NW, Suite 1200
Washington, DC 20005

(202) 296-5469
website: www.tobaccofreekids.org

The Campaign for Tobacco-Free Kids is a nonprofit organization that aims to reduce tobacco use and its deadly toll in the United States and around the world. It advocates for public policies proven to prevent kids from smoking, help smokers quit, and protect everyone from secondhand smoke. On its website, the organization offers fact sheets on tobacco as well as information about issues such as regulation, taxation, sales, and labeling of these products.

Citizens for Tobacco Rights

www.tobaccorights.com

Citizens for Tobacco Rights helps adult smokers and dippers stay informed about tobacco issues and learn how to become effective legislative advocates. It is supported by Philip Morris USA, US Smokeless Tobacco Company, and John Middleton. The group's website provides information on important tobacco issues such as taxes and regulation, encourages adult tobacco consumers to get involved in the legislative and regulatory process, and helps adult tobacco consumers become effective legislative advocates and make their voices heard.

Competitive Enterprise Institute (CEI)

1899 L Street NW, 12th Floor
Washington, DC 20036
(202) 331-1010 • fax: (202) 331-0640
e-mail: info@cei.org
website: www.cei.org

CEI is a public interest group dedicated to free enterprise and limited government. CEI questions the validity and accuracy of Environmental Protection Agency studies that report the dangers of secondhand smoke. Its publications include policy studies and several newsletters, including *CEI Planet*, in which the recent article, "Congress, Tobacco, and a President Who Lights Up," appeared.

Heartland Institute

One South Wacker Drive #2740
Chicago, IL 60606
(312) 377-4000 • fax: (312)377-5000
e-mail: think@heartland.org
website: http://heartland.org

Founded in 1984, the Heartland Institute is a nonprofit research and education organization with the mission to discover, develop, and promote free-market solutions to social and economic problems. The institute advocates for smokers' rights, charging antismoking groups with using propaganda and exaggerations to promote tobacco control. On its website, its Smoking Lounge provides information for tobacco users, covering issues such as smoking bans, taxes, and secondhand smoke. The Heartland Institute also published a book defending smokers, *Please Don't Poop in My Salad*.

National Youth Rights Association (NYRA)

1101 15th Street NW, Suite 200
Washington, DC 20005
(202) 835-1739
website: www.youthrights.org

The National Youth Rights Association is a youth-led national non-profit organization dedicated to fighting for the civil rights and liberties of young people. NYRA has more than seven thousand members representing all fifty states. It seeks to lower the voting age, lower the drinking age, repeal curfew laws, and protect student rights.

truth

website: www.thetruth.com

Funded by the American Legacy Foundation, the truth campaign focuses on the tobacco industry, alleging that it manipulates its products, research, and advertising to secure replacements for the smokers that quit and die every day in the United States. Its website offers information on the tobacco industry as well as sections dedicated to music, games, sports, and a blog.

US Food and Drug Administration (FDA)

10903 New Hampshire Avenue
Silver Spring, MD 20993
(888) INFO-FDA (463-6332)
website: www.fda.gov

The FDA is one of the nation's oldest consumer protection agencies. Its mission is to promote and protect the public health by helping safe and effective products reach the market in a timely way; monitor products for continued safety after they are in use; and help the public get the accurate, science-based information needed to improve health. On the FDA's website, its section on tobacco products offers information on marketing and labeling of tobacco, electronic cigarettes, youth smoking, and other issues.

For Further Reading

Books

Joseph L. Bast, *Please Don't Poop in My Salad*. Chicago: Heartland Institute, 2006.

Allan M. Brandt, *The Cigarette Century: The Rise, Fall, and Deadly Persistence of the Product That Defined America*. New York: Basic Books, 2007.

Eric Burns, *The Smoke of the Gods: A Social History of Tobacco*. Philadelphia: Temple University Press, 2007.

Martha A. Derthick, *Up in Smoke: From Legislation to Litigation in Tobacco Politics* (third edition). Washington, DC: CQ Press, 2012.

Sharon Y. Eubanks and Stanton A. Glantz, *Bad Acts: The Racketeering Case Against the Tobacco Industry*. Washington, DC: American Public Health Association, 2012.

Iain Gately, *Tobacco: A Cultural History of How an Exotic Plant Seduced Civilization*. New York: Grove Press, 2002.

Sander L. Gilman and Zhou Xun, eds., *Smoke: A Global History of Smoking*. London, UK: Reaktion Books, 2004.

Robert N. Proctor, *Golden Holocaust: Origins of the Cigarette Catastrophe and the Case for Abolition*. Berkeley: University of California Press, 2011.

Clete Snell, *Peddling Poison: The Tobacco Industry and Kids*. Westport, CN: Praeger, 2005.

Christopher Snowdon, *Velvet Glove, Iron Fist: A History of Anti-Smoking*. Ripon, UK: Little Dice, 2009.

Dan Zegart, *Civil Warriors: The Legal Siege on the Tobacco Industry*. New York: Delacorate Press, 2000.

Periodicals

Steve Chapman, "Sweet Lies About Kids and Smoking," *Reason*, September 28, 2009.

Myra Fleischer, "Smokers Losing Child Custody Cases a Growing Trend," *Washington Times*, February 21, 2012.

Roxanne Khamsi, "Smoking Is a Drag at the Box Office," *Scientific American*, October 10, 2011.

Abbey Lewis, "Cracking the Flavor Code," *CSP Magazine*, December 2009.

Los Angeles Times, "A Smoke-Free UC Goes Too Far," January 18, 2012.

John Luik, "Monkey See, Monkey Do?," *Tobacco Reporter*, August 2007.

Patti Neighmond, "One Teen's Struggle to Quit," www.npr.org, November 6, 2008.

Michael B. Siegel, "A Smoking Ban Too Far," *New York Times*, May 5, 2011.

Julie Carr Smyth, "Colleges May Ban Smoking," *Salon*, June 28, 2012.

Christopher Snowdon, "Smoking Ban Health Miracle Is a Myth," *Heartlander*, January 19, 2010.

Index